The Trinity Mystery

The Trinity Mystery

Discovering the Doctrine of the Trinity
and Its Implications

SAM ANDERSEN

WIPF & STOCK · Eugene, Oregon

THE TRINITY MYSTERY
Discovering the Doctrine of the Trinity and Its Implications

Wipf & Stock
An Imprint of Wipf and Stock Publishers
199 W. 8th Ave., Suite 3
Eugene, OR 97401

www.wipfandstock.com

PAPERBACK ISBN: 978-1-6667-3213-9
HARDCOVER ISBN: 978-1-6667-2547-6
EBOOK ISBN: 978-1-6667-2548-3

DECEMBER 16, 2021

For

EFCO

Contents

Bible Version Abbreviations

NASB	New American Standard Bible. La Habra: Lockman Foundation, 1995.
NIV	New International Version. Kenneth Barker et al. Grand Rapids: Zondervan, 2002.
NKJV	New King James Version. Nashville: Thomas Nelson, 1997.
RSV	Revised Standard Version. Edited by Herbert G. May and Bruce M. Metzger. New York: Oxford University Press, 1977.

Introduction

GOOD BOOKS DO NOT NEED an apology, so let me give you an excuse for why this book was written. It all began when one of our church elders asked whether I would like to preach one sermon in a series about the attributes of God. What came to my mind were God's omniscience, omnipotence, and omnipresence, but then I figured that someone must want to talk about the wrath of God. It is a topic that receives too little attention by most Christians and is perhaps a subject of guilty pleasure for others. Not being particularly inclined to speak on any of these, and not understanding what the underlying purpose for the series was, I half-jokingly suggested the Trinity.

What a foolish thing to say! Why? Because my elder said, "Okay, sounds good."

Right then and there I realized the terrible nature of my situation. Having grown up in evangelical churches, I fully accepted the confession that God is Trinitarian. I could state, without hesitation, that Father, Son, and Spirit are God. I might even be able to quote some scriptures that would prove Jesus is God, but I had never thought about why the Holy Spirit is considered God. I did not even know if there was a catch-all passage where the Trinity is clearly taught. Needless to say I had a great deal of work ahead of me if I was to do justice to my topic.

As I dug deeper and deeper it became apparent that there was far too much material to cram into a thirty to forty minute period. What's more, I was becoming engrossed in my subject. I was not just gathering information to vomit back out at the congregation. There was something here, something deeply moving and illuminating. It was a most startling thing. And when at last I stood before the congregation and spoke far longer than perhaps was comfortable for most people, I had only barely scratched the surface of this important doctrine. When I stopped speaking, stepped down, and returned to my seat, I felt that what I had said was thoroughly inadequate. Oh, certainly I had stated that it was within the context of the Trinity that all the other attributes were to be understood, but stating is different than describing.

If my preaching that day did nothing else it fueled my own desire to better understand this subject. Fortunately, I had finished my graduate work a few months before, and was waiting eagerly for a college to accept my resume and hire me on as a history teacher. So, as my resume floated in the waters of the job market like a bobber at the end of a fishing line, I set about doing some light studying on the Trinity. It was not an aggressive study, because deadlines were a thing of the past. But then the pastor of our church announced his retirement.

Weeks turned to months without a single interview. Being caught in one of life's in-between places is not an enjoyable thing, but that is where I found myself. So I flippantly told God that I was willing to do whatever it was he wanted me to. I made an offer to the church elders: I would prepare a series of twelve sermons on the doctrine of the Trinity if they needed someone to provide some fill-in preaching. And, having made this formal offer, I set myself to study in earnest, and to consider how to present what I was learning.

This book is the fruit of that work. It is certainly not the most original or the most scholarly or even the simplest book on the subject. Nevertheless I will appeal to the spirit of Augustine in that, though there are certainly numerous other works on this subject, it may be that a few people will begin with this book, find here a sufficiently different perspective that brings clarity to some truth, or which may bring to mind some interesting questions that lead to deeper contemplation. As Augustine said, "It is useful that many persons should write many books, differing in style but not in faith, concerning even the same questions, that the matter itself may reach the greatest number—some in one way, some in another."[1]

What may be of some interest to readers is the method in which the doctrine of the Trinity is approached here. Instead of offering a systematic style, I offer the unraveling of a mystery. It is the mystery of how the church has arrived at such a bizarre conclusion concerning God—a conclusion which for many is difficult to understand and for most is difficult to explain. It is a conclusion that is to some (such as Muslims) both startling and blasphemous. But it is a conclusion that is a deduction from evidence.

---

1. Augustine, *On the Trinity*, 1.3.5

The biblical data is like the dead body in a locked room. How did the body get there and how was the person killed? And what are we supposed to do with it?

It is my hope that in presenting the Trinity in this way I can share with you some of the joy of doing theology. It really is a marvelous thing to think about what God has revealed about himself. I mean actually thinking about it and not just passively receiving it. There is something frustrating and yet deeply satisfying in being able to know how you arrive at a theological conclusion. There is great joy in being led down the words of the Spirit to find a description of God there: not just that he is there, but the peculiarities of his nature and that in studying you have discovered him. It is not that you are the first one to do so, but that you *have* done so. It is like a person seeing the sea after a lifetime of living in the Midwest of the United States. "I have heard of You by the hearing of the ear, but now my eye sees You," is what Job said when at last God appeared.[2] We may say something similar when for ourselves we see in scripture what manner of God lives.

It is also my hope that, in presenting more of a pastoral style as opposed to a systematic one, the reader might not only come to grips with the doctrine itself, but also with its implications. For it has been one of the most surprising things to me that the doctrine of the Trinity not only touches on every part of Christian theology, but it also informs numerous other aspects of life: from love, to ideas of origin, movement, and motivation, even to concepts of communication. The Trinity stands at the center of the Christian faith, life, and practice. It is the unifying principle in all of Christian theology, anthropology, and general philosophy. While I do not claim to be a skilled enough writer and thinker to actually lay out all these things in a deep and meaningful way, I do hope to whet your appetite. For I am convinced that this is the highest and most beautiful revelation God has made about himself. It is a privilege to live in just such a time, just such an age that he has made this revelation, for in ages past he did not so reveal himself even to the chosen people of Israel. I therefore invite you to put on your detective's cap, pull out your theological magnifying glass, and examine the evidence. Be convinced for yourself of the wonderful truth of God which he has revealed.

---

2. Job 42:5 (Unless otherwise stated, I will be using the NKJV).

1

The Hand of God at Work

"I had always felt life first as a story: and if there is a story
there is a story-teller."

—G.K. Chesterton[1]

ONE OF THE GREATEST mystery novels in English literature is the *Hound of the Baskervilles*. That story begins not with a dead body, but with the appearance of James Mortimer at the rooms of 221b Baker Street. Upon his arrival the poor man proceeds to explain the history of the Baskerville curse, starting at the beginning of everything so that Sherlock Holmes might come to the correct deduction and solve the case. Our own mystery must proceed along the same lines. We must, theologically speaking, start at the beginning. That beginning is not monotheism.

Believe me, I cringe at the thought of saying that, but it really is a true statement. The most basic question humans ask are not how many gods are there. Instead, we ask why the world works and how the world works. I mean this in a very real way. Every day things happen, and not because you or I or another human being does anything. Take rain, for example. How would you describe the cause and origin of the rain? Some of you reading this are really on top of it! You've got the weather app on your phone, or you might turn to the local news station to watch the meteorologist point at a green-screen. You know all about high pressures and low pressures.

1. Chesterton, *Orthodoxy*, 264.

You might even understand the concept of El Niño—that mysterious thing that seems to be the cause of everything and nothing related to climate. You might even plan your day on what the forecast is. Why? Because you believe we know how the world works. The assumption is that weather works according to certain principles and physical laws, and that same assumption extends to the rest of the world. Farmers do certain things to their fields in order to maximize crop yield: ensuring proper drainage, fertilizing, spraying herbicides or insecticides, or by choosing a particular seed strain. Or, if you're a fan of astronomy, you know that scientists have calculated the movements of the planets. They can tell you where Mars or Uranus will be at any time of the year or for any number of years. Actually, it was because Uranus was not quite following the orbital path astronomers had calculated that they were able to discover the existence of Neptune.[2]

These kinds of things, these rules by which the universe operates, are probably best described as *natural laws*. The weather, the planets, the workings of the human body, and everything else function in ways that are generally predictable. Of course naturalists and materialists would say that it is laws all the way—from galactic structures to the quantum realm. No matter how big or how small there will always be a fundamental way any given thing or system will operate. Matter and energy function according to these principles because in order to exist as they are they must act in this way. To the people who hold this position the child-like question of *why* must inevitably be given the answer which is fundamentally adultish: *because that's the way it is.*

This concept of reality is strange in that it is fairly new in human history, but it has been adopted by most materialists and many Christians in the western world. The materialist will look around and say there is no God, that matter and energy are all that exist, ever has existed, and ever will exist.[3] The Christian, on the other hand, sees the signs of a Creator everywhere. The apparent design in the systems of the universe are proof of a Designer. Storms work a particular way because God caused the specific physical forces to work the way they do. It is rather like a machine, a computer for instance. A computer is designed to function a certain way depending on what data it receives. If someone opens a word processor and begins to type, then letters and words are going to appear on screen. Install a program to open when the computer turns on and that is exactly what

2. Glover et al., *National Geographic Encyclopedia of Space*, 164.

3. Sire, *Universe Next Door*, 66–93.

will happen. Whenever you need to forcibly close a program, control + alt + delete is the go-to key selection for a Microsoft machine. Do you need your computer to stop working completely? Throw it against a wall or drop it in a lake. If a person does these things a predicable outcome will occur.

Most Christians seem to have this understanding of the world.[4] We see mechanisms and laws acting on their own but because they clearly are mechanisms and laws then we cannot help but say that this is evidence for God. Christians make a big deal out of this. Entire apologetic institutions have been created in order to prove that God is the programmer. Entire atheistic organizations have been founded in order to argue that the world works because the world has always worked. Both of these camps understand something very important, and it is this: At the foundation of all knowledge, of all wisdom, of all purpose, all morality and practice is the question of God and the universe. Everything, even from the atheistic perspective, has a theological (or anti-theological) basis.

PLAINLY VISIBLE

This, then, is where we must start our investigation into the Trinity. It is not in arguing whether or not God exists. As we shall see, I do not think that really has to be proved. Rather, we must start by understanding what exactly the Bible means when it presents a living and active God. To do this we cannot start with our own assumptions, but must consider how ancient man understood God to be working in the world. This is touched on in Romans 1:18–25.

> For the wrath of God is revealed from heaven against all ungodliness and unrighteousness of men, who suppress the truth in unrighteousness, because what may be known of God is manifest in them, for God has shown it to them. For since the creation of the world His invisible attributes are clearly seen, being understood by the things that are made, even His eternal power and Godhead, so that they are without excuse, because, although they knew God, they did not glorify Him as God, nor were thankful, but became futile in their thoughts, and their foolish hearts were darkened.

4. Sire, *Universe Next Door*, 25–46. Sire differentiates the Theistic universe from the Deistic one by specifying the openness of the former and closed nature of the latter; and by the continued involvement of God in the former and the hands-off approach of God in the latter. However, it has been my experience that most Christians function in a sort of in-between place.

Professing to be wise, they became fools, and changed the glory of the incorruptible God into an image made like corruptible man— and birds and four-footed animals and creeping things. Therefore God also gave them up to uncleanness, in the lusts of their hearts, to dishonor their bodies among themselves, who exchanged the truth of God for the lie, and worshiped and served the creature rather than the Creator, who is blessed forever. Amen.

Paul's intent in the letter to the Romans seems to be twofold. First, he desires to present the gospel to the Romans. This is rather interesting in itself, considering the fact that his readers were already disciples of Christ. So he could not mean what generally comes to our mind: a sort of bare bones gospel of Christ having died and rose again. What Paul meant was something bigger and he provides a grand discussion of the gospel in this letter. His purpose was to help the church better understand this good news and what the implications were for their lives, including their interactions with other people—especially Jews. And intertwined with all of this is Paul's second purpose: for the Roman church to help him along to Spain.

It is with these things in mind that Paul begins the letter, explaining that he has been tasked to preach the gospel to the Gentiles. He is not ashamed of this message he gives, even though it puts him into terrible and shameful situations: fraternizing with Gentiles, prison, and stoning just to name a few. But he was not ashamed. Why? Because he understood his gospel to be the power of God unto salvation. Salvation from what? Salvation from the wrath of God. This is the key. Sometimes we forget what we are saved from. Paul makes it clear that the righteous live by faith, and those who are righteous are not under wrath, but it is wrath which Paul addresses. He says that the wrath of God is revealed from heaven already because man is suppressing that which can be known of God: his eternal power and godhead, as the New King James puts it.

Just what is meant by these two terms? First, eternal power is not something in the past. Sometimes we think of God in this way: that he expended a great deal of energy to create the world and has been watching it go ever since. That's not what eternal power means. It is at once a thing past, present, and future. This invisible attribute is clearly seen in the world around us, but it is not an echo, like the background radiation we find in the universe. This is a power that was used and is being used even now.

The second thing Paul mentions is God's *theiotes*, what the New King James calls the *godhead* and which really means God's divine nature. It is

4

not so much what makes God to be God, as in omnipotence, omnipresence, etc. Instead, this seems to be the revelation *of* God, that there is a deity who is at work and made known by this work. We are not looking at the aftermath of some divine act. It is something alive right now and active right now. We should see it. We should recognize it. And according to verse 21 we should glorify him and be thankful to him because he is God.

What is remarkable about this is that Paul is not making an argument for the existence of God. He says that evidence is already visible, and what's more, it is recognized by men. God has manifested it to men, meaning it is so clear and obvious that it *is* known, not merely that it can be discovered. He is not hiding in the dark places of the world waiting for someone to happen along and say, "Oh, hello, God, didn't know you were there. How nice to find you at last!" The evidence of God's existence is not a mere philosophical conclusion either. No, he is there, and, as the title of Francis Shaeffer's book has it, he is not silent. God is there, and this is known by every single one of us, believer and unbeliever alike. This is what is meant by verse 19 which reads, "Because what may be known of God is manifest in them, for God has shown it to them." The "them" here are humans in general. Everyone knows the existence and power of God. It is beyond doubt for all people.

This has important implications. First, it makes futile the efforts by some people to prove or disprove the existence of God. Paul is clear that that the world around us reveals there is divinity and that this divinity has a power which is absolute and eternal. This truth is known, and trying to prove it would be like proving the sky is blue, or that zebras have stripes, or that you have a nose on your face. You're trying to prove something so obvious that it really doesn't need proving. When people say they just can't believe in God or that there isn't enough evidence for him, these people are *choosing* not to believe their eyes. They are rejecting what they know to be true. It is an experiential knowledge more intimate that any schooling can offer because it is the education of living. When we choose to not only suppress this truth but also not to be thankful to the one whose eternal power and existence is evidenced by our continued lives, then God takes the next step and reveals his wrath to these people.

This rejection of God is certainly applicable to our modern tendency to push God out of every venue—politics, science, history, work, in doing the laundry, or buying groceries, or simply resting—but Paul does not go to atheism in his description of what occurs. It is true that the fool says in his heart there is no God, but Paul speaks of a different kind of darkening of the heart. He speaks of a twisting and corrupting. The people described in Romans knew God and corrupted their understanding of who should receive glory and thanks. They corrupted him, or at least corrupted him in their own minds by worshiping created things: the sun, moon, earth, birds, animals, even fellow human beings, or some barbarous compilation of two or more of these. Part of what Paul describes is idolatry which, if you remember, was what Israel did when Moses was a long time coming back down the mountain. They created a golden calf and it is interesting what Aaron said about it. He said, "This is your god, O Israel, that brought you out of the land of Egypt." And again after building an altar he said, "Tomorrow is a feast to the LORD."[5] In the minds of the Israelites they were, to some extent, serving the same deity who had brought them out of Egypt. They had merely given him form, a shape, a sign of his presence. And this, Paul says in Romans 1, is what corrupt men do, but I think there is another part to it.

The sin Paul had in mind is not just creating an image to represent the invisible God. Paul says they really did begin to worship things that were not divine. Not only did they elevate created things to the level of God, but they twisted their understanding of the divine nature. They tried to take God down, or at least his divinity, and desecrated it in their understanding. No longer was God one and eternally powerful. The one God became many gods, and their powers were specific, tied to the working of the world. These gods were given characteristics which were not holy or divine: weakness, gullibility, failure, lust, and various other things that define men. In a sort of corrupt incarnation the gods became like men, even if they did not come in the true form and appearance of a man.

The awe ancient men had for the divine, though twisted, did fulfill part of what Paul said men's attitudes should be like. They *did* perceive the divine hand at work, though to them it was not one or even two hands, but many. In a sense this is good, because it does something that those of us in the west fail to do. They saw the evidence of God as present in an active exercising of power, not, as we do, in the marks of apparent design in creation. Our perspective is a forensic one, theirs was experiential—not of natural, dumb forces, but of personality and power.

5. Exod 32:4–5.

A WORLD OF PERSONALITY AND POWER

It is difficult to appreciate this point of view. To say that the ancients looked at the universe and saw personality is to say something very strange. What does it mean? It means that when man looked around he was overcome by a sense of power at work. If he looked at the sun, for instance, he did not see a ball of gas ninety-three million miles away running on a fusion reaction. Instead, depending on his culture, he likely saw it as a being fiercely alive in the sky, much, much closer than ninety-three million miles. To such a man, the sun has moods: at times merely providing life-giving light and warmth, but at other times directing his fierce face toward the earth with such intensity that he withers crops and strikes men dead. Even in modern times there are those who worship the sun. Rabi R. Maharaj recalls a time when, prior to his conversion to Christianity, he would regularly worship the sun by staring at it for long periods of time with eyes wide open, believing completely that it had the "power of saving the soul fully devoted to it."[6]

Aside from the sun the ancient worldview perceived numerous other powers at work. Rivers, for example, were not merely water running along a well worn path. *The Iliad* records how the mighty hero Achilles battled the river Xanthos. The river was filled with rage as the Greek slew Trojan warrior after Trojan warrior along his banks until at last the river "cold with rage, in likeness of a man, assumed a voice and spoke from a whirlpool" telling Achilles to stop. When the man refused the river surged, rising up to overwhelm the Greek warrior. It was only by an act of the god Hephaestus, who brought a roaring fire to battle the raging waters, that the river was turned back.[7] Then there are storms, and many nations around the Mediterranean acknowledged the existence of storm gods: Zeus of the Greeks, Iškur of the Sumerians, Adad of Assyrians and Babylonians, or Ba'al of biblical fame. And if anyone needs an explanation for why men would attribute storms to gods, then he need only step out in a storm. As the wind howls and tries to knock you down and rain blasts your face, what reaction would you have? Is it not an overwhelming fear to rush inside? Or perhaps it is defiance: a desire to shake your fist at the wind and say, "Is that all you've got?" Our mind tells us it is merely a process, merely physics and chemistry working together, but the feeling is of personality.

6. Maharaj, *Death of a Guru*, 53.
7. Homer, *The Iliad*, book 21.

The ancients took storms just as seriously as we do, but from a different starting point. Today, if a storm threatened, you would take shelter, and if you were a farmer you would hope that your drainage system was sufficient, and that your crops were rooted enough to withstand the winds. If you are a Christian you might pray something like, *God, please don't let it be too bad!* But you would never treat the storm as a person, and it is highly likely that you would not think the storm an act of God. The weather channel would inform you of high and low pressures, warm fronts and cold fronts: each of them impersonal forces of nature. But if we had the perspective of the ancients, then it would be quite acceptable and proper for the weather man to speak of Thor smiting the Midwest. He might suggest that instead of taking shelter farmers should sacrifice the fatted calf. If things got really bad, then the National Weather Service might order the town virgins to be brought out and offered as a sacrifice. This might seem funny and farcical, but the ancients did not think so. Archeologists have found administrative texts from the city of Ur which addressed what should be done when a storm approached. Certain rights were to be performed in order to appease the god Iškur so that the storm would pass by or cause little damage.[8] To the people and government of Ur, storms were not natural things devoid of meaning and personality, but were the acts of someone powerful and were incredibly serious. Performing the proper rituals could mean life or death for the individual, family, or for the city.

Again, this seems strange to us because we start from a different vantage point. We are surprised when deity shows up for anything. Even when we talk about God acting, it is almost as if his actions were a surprise and extraordinary. Not so the ancients or those who hold to the most ancient worldview systems. In their experience, the universe was and is alive all around them. "Powers confront man wherever he move[d]" and they could be recognized in a variety of ways.[9] Imagine a village where one of the men goes and finds a curious bit of metal. He brings it home, rather like you or I might bring home an interesting rock. But then, not many days later, the man falls ill. It is just at this point where worldviews diverge. We would think the rock is radioactive or that a disease is carried on its surface. The ancients would have assumed there was a god in or about the bit of metal, and the only way to heal the man would be to appease the god. So the

8. Schwemer, "Storm-Gods of the Ancient Near East," 132.

9. Frankfort, *Ancient Egyptian Religion*, 4–5. (The example I give is a slightly modified version of the one Frankfort provides in his book.)

village would erect a shrine and bring offerings to the god of the metal. At some point it would no longer matter whether the man lived or died. He might live if the god was appeased, or he might die because his sin was so egregious. What is important in this illustration is that the village would take it for granted that the divine could and would dwell in the same geographic area as themselves and have an effect on the world. To them, it was not a matter of something from outside the world-system reaching in (like we would think of as a miracle) because such things happened regularly. As Paul Hiebert puts it, "In such a world, no distinction is made between the supernatural and the natural."[10]

The best way I know how to really get a grip on this is through fairy tales. In most fairy tales there is a combination of the real and the imaginary, but the conjunction is seamless and natural, even if it is startling. Just consider C.S. Lewis's *Chronicles of Narnia* which offers a sort of baptized paganism. It is a world filled with talking beasts and dwarfs, and with dryads and naiads, the gods and goddesses of the trees and rivers. Even the very trees are alive and listening. All of this is a very strange thing for anyone entering Narnia because life and personality are everywhere, taking unexpected shapes, and people needed to be on guard for it. Mr. Beaver's warning to the children that the trees are always listening is a good example. He says, "Most of them are on our side, but there *are* trees that would betray us to *her*."[11]

This is exactly the type of world the ancients perceived. It was a world filled with life and the divine. Certainly we should reject their belief in many gods, and can question whether all storms are the work of an angered deity. But can the seriousness of our forefathers be so easily dismissed? Recall the city of Ur which was so serious about storms that the government established what rites needed to be performed. Do you know who came from Ur? The patriarch Abraham came from that city. And we should not think that he was like us in every respect, for he was closer to that worldview than to ours.

This type of world we have been discussing was familiar to the patriarchs, the Israelites, and the early church. It was the perspective Paul describes when he says that the power and divinity of God is evident all around, and it is exactly this thing which was twisted. He was not criticizing them for seeing power at work, only that they were attributing these divine

10. Heibert, *Transforming Worldviews*, 106.
11. Lewis, *Lion, the Witch, and the Wardrobe*, 234.

things to undivine things. This is the point I am trying to make, and the reason we have spent so much time on this. Paul does not criticize the fact that they perceived personal power at work. Their sin was to reject the truth of who was at work, and to twist their understanding of his nature.

Notice how different this is from our predisposition. We agree with the Bible that the sun, moon, and stars are not personal powers themselves. We agree with the Bible that the trees, rocks, or pieces of metal do not contain God. But we go too far when we say that God pokes his finger every once in a while into a world that would otherwise get along fairly well on its own. This attitude is completely foreign to that which has been held by most of humanity for most of history. It sucks the life out of existence. It tears apart the world, which was once a seamless cloth, into such spheres of influence as spiritual and physical, natural and supernatural, religious or secular.[12] The cultures of the ancient world would never have made this division, and I include in this the ancient and thoroughly truthful perspective offered by the Bible.

THE BIBLICAL PERSPECTIVE

The Bible presents God as more than the Creator—at least in the sense that we usually mean creator. When we use the word, often we think that creation is, in a sense, independent. We think of a LEGO creation or a computer. The Creator assembles, programs, and then lets go. But when describing God, the Bible goes beyond the idea of merely assembling. It goes beyond starting something up and letting it go. God is never as distant as this would imply, and we are not so independent as we might hope.

Leviticus 14:33–53 is a passage which illustrates this. It is a straightforward, if strange text, that because of its position in the Bible, many Christians probably read through rather quickly—after all, there are few books in the Bible as tedious as Leviticus! The passage contains guidelines for when a house becomes leprous. Leprosy seems to have been a sort of catch-all for several different problems which affected both the house for the soul and the house for the body. In this particular case, *leprosy* is referring to some kind of mold or mildew.

> And the LORD SPOKE TO MOSES AND AARON, SAYING: "When you have come into the land of Canaan, which I give you as a

12. Walton, *Ancient Near Eastern Thought*, 87.

possession, and I put the leprous plague in a house in the land of your possession, and he who owns the house comes and tells the priest, saying, 'It seems to me that *there is* some plague in the house,' then the priest shall command that they empty the house, before the priest goes *into it* to examine the plague, that all that *is* in the house may not be made unclean; and afterward the priest shall go in to examine the house. And he shall examine the plague; and indeed *if* the plague *is* on the walls of the house with ingrained streaks, greenish or reddish, which appear to be deep in the wall, then the priest shall go out of the house, to the door of the house, and shut up the house seven days. And the priest shall come again on the seventh day and look; and indeed *if* the plague has spread on the walls of the house, then the priest shall command that they take away the stones in which *is* the plague, and they shall cast them into an unclean place outside the city. And he shall cause the house to be scraped inside, all around, and the dust that they scrape off they shall pour out in an unclean place outside the city. Then they shall take other stones and put *them* in the place of *those* stones, and he shall take other mortar and plaster the house. Now if the plague comes back and breaks out in the house, after he has taken away the stones, after he has scraped the house, and after it is plastered, then the priest shall come and look; and indeed *if* the plague has spread in the house, it *is* an active leprosy in the house. It *is* unclean. And he shall break down the house, its stones, its timber, and all the plaster of the house, and he shall carry *them* outside the city to an unclean place. Moreover he who goes into the house at all while it is shut up shall be unclean until evening. And he who lies down in the house shall wash his clothes, and he who eats in the house shall wash his clothes.

But if the priest comes in and examines *it,* and indeed the plague has not spread in the house after the house was plastered, then the priest shall pronounce the house clean, because the plague is healed. And he shall take, to cleanse the house, two birds, cedar wood, scarlet, and hyssop. Then he shall kill one of the birds in an earthen vessel over running water; and he shall take the cedar wood, the hyssop, the scarlet, and the living bird, and dip them in the blood of the slain bird and in the running water, and sprinkle the house seven times. And he shall cleanse the house with the blood of the bird and the running water and the living bird, with the cedar wood, the hyssop, and the scarlet. Then he shall let the living bird loose outside the city in the open field, and make atonement for the house, and it shall be clean.

The whole thing seems rather odd and unscientific, doesn't it? I don't think it is the kind of cleaning procedure that would be recommended by your local home improvement expert. And why were priests involved? I have heard it said that they were the most educated people in the nation, so they were the closest thing the Israelites had to doctors or scientists. But I don't want you to focus on that aspect; instead, focus on one little verse: verse 34. It reads, "When you enter the land of Canaan, which I give you for a possession, and I put a mark of leprosy on a house in the land of your possession . . ." Do you notice who put the leprosy on the house? It is God. He takes responsibility for this little thing, this little impurity which could result in the destruction of an entire house! He does not say that in the natural course of events that some leprosy might appear on the primitive house wall. He does not say that it was caused by a microbial infection or fungus. He says, "When . . . I put a mark of leprosy on a house." Which worldview does this seem to align with?

Next, consider the book of Job, specifically the sections where God speaks. In chapter 38 God describes the founding of the earth and that the boundaries were set for the sea. These things are put in the past, but then God asks Job something from the present, and the NASB puts it rather bluntly. God asks, "Have you ever in your life commanded the morning and caused it to know its place, that it might take hold of the ends of the earth and the wicked be shaken out of it?"[13]

I just love that. "Have you *ever in your life*?!" Has the sun ever gone up because Job told it to? Has he ever used it to catch the wicked in the act and the punish them? Has the sun ever served Job in this way? The answer, of course, is no. But there is another part to the answer. It is the assumption that cannot be avoided, and it is the one we readily agree with. At the same time it is an assumption we too often forget when we actually look at a sunrise. I don't mean just looking at one, but actually thinking about what is going on. We have been taught, truthfully enough I suppose, that when we see a sunrise it is because the Earth is rotating so different parts of the planet are exposed to sunlight. It really does happen that way, but at the same time it is not what it sounds like. The Earth does not just spin because that is what the Earth does. It spins because God causes it to do so. It is not that he *caused* it to start spinning, but each time it completes a revolution it is because God has commanded *that* revolution. Every single turn, every single sunrise is at the command of God. This is the other answer to the

13. Job 38:12–14

question posed to Job. Who causes the sun to rise each and every time and for his own purpose? God does.

A few verses later in Job, God asks, "Who has divided a channel for the overflowing water, or a path for the thunderbolt to cause it to rain on a land where there is no one, a wilderness in which there is no man; to satisfy the desolate waste, and to cause to spring forth the growth of tender grass?"[14] Consider what is being said here. The question is not *what* causes the water to flow a certain way. The question is not *what* causes the bolt of lightning to go from one place to another. Those are the kinds of questions we ask. We look for mechanisms, not personality. But look at how the questions are framed in Job. It is not a question of *what* but of *whom*! And look at the detail! The flowing of electrons from one precise point to another is what God commands. And he causes it to happen every time.

God is also the one who causes it to rain in a place where no man lives. In this way he laughs at the philosophers who wonder whether there is a world outside of man's perception. Here God makes it clear that where man's sight and abilities are limited his are not, and he causes grass to grow where a lawnmower will never touch. As Psalm 104:10–18 describes, God gives water for the beasts of the field. He makes a home for the birds and the goats and the badgers. The animal kingdom does not function on its own. God provides for it! The livelihood of an insect in the middle of the South American jungle—a creature no man has seen and never will see—gets its daily life from the hand of God. Man has cataloged numerous species of creatures, but there are many, many more he knows nothing about, and yet God cares for them.

God gives to every creature what he desires. There is not a dog that has enjoyed a bone, not a cat that enjoyed catnip, not a horse that has enjoyed a roll in the grass that was not given by the hand of God. There is not a man or woman on earth who lives, no matter how meagerly, except by the hand of God. Every sunrise, every raindrop, every strike of lightning, every piece of bread, every drink of water is yours because he gives it to you.

Our temptation is to perceive all these things, what might be call the natural world, as working on their own as mechanical things. We see processes when we ought to see personality. This is no mere religious sentiment. It is not about religion at all. It is about the world itself. It is about life itself. Recognizing the processes at work is not wrong, but we must not forget that behind the process someone is working.

14. Job 38:25–30

ADDRESSING TODAY

The sin the ancients committed was in worshiping the creation instead of the Creator. They made idols and multiplied gods for themselves because they refused to see the one God at work. The biblical revelation corrects this. It says no, there are not thousands or millions of gods at work. There is only one. This revelation sweeps aside all of the junk until only the truth remains. It straightens out the world, but does not break it.

Our modern view, on the other hand, shatters the world. The atheistic part of our culture points out that the Bible does away with all the other gods—millions of gods, perhaps. The only difference between the atheistic worldview and ours is one—one God. The Israelites were constantly tempted by those other cultures to turn from the one to the many. The difference between one and a million is a million. Our culture calls on us to turn from the one to the none. But the difference between one and none is everything. It is incalculable. It is the world.

The atheistic perspective has no room for a divine being at work in the cosmos. Everything is because everything is. There are natural laws by which everything functions and those laws exist because they must exist. The universe would not work if the cosmological constant was different, or if gravity did not work, or the atomic forces were even a little different. Therefore, to them, the universe works because it could not be any other way. Everything, from the largest galaxy to the smallest quanta, runs on some kind of rule. Animals live and die based on a combination of biological necessity and the actions of chemistry and physics. The world's weather is subject to many different variables and is a carefully balanced affair. The sun does not really rise and set, but we can be sure that for billions of years to come, Earth will rotate on its axis and cause different parts of its surface to be exposed to light. Why? Because the Earth is in motion and will stay in motion until stopped. To think that a special ritual must be performed so that the sun will rise, or to believe that we must appease a deity to get a storm to pass, is complete ignorance. Not only that, but it is detrimental to society, to knowledge, and the betterment of humanity. After all, meteorology, not sacrifice, protects countless lives by giving storm warnings.

Think about that for a moment. While it is flavored with an atheistic worldview, does it sound so dissimilar to how many of us perceive the world? We would agree with very nearly every point of it. We only make room for *miracles*: "an interference with Nature by supernatural power."[15] Nature works well enough on its own, and God only sometimes interferes.

The problem with describing the world in this way is that it deprives existence of life and personality. Yes, the world does seem to work this way: from the turning of the Earth, to warm and cold fronts colliding to make storms. But it is, at the same time, insufficient. It is like saying that eating is the shoving of foreign substances into a hole in one's head.[16] It is technically accurate, but it is woefully inadequate. More than that, it takes a human thing and transforms it into something grotesque. It removes all personality from the act.

The only reason we perceive the world in this way is because we do not have a proper view of God's eternal power and divinity. We look for God in the big things, to reach down and do the seemingly impossible. In other words, we look for him to do the supernatural, to do something unexpected. Rarely do we see him at work in the mundane, in the ordinary, and in the expected.

We make a great and grave mistake when perceiving God this way. It is like we have put on blinders so that all the things that are not big and impossible are, well, plain, everyday, and ordinary. They are expected. They are expected, in fact, rather like you would expect a waiter to bring food or drink at a restaurant. What is curious about a waiter in a restaurant, is that for most of the dining experience we try to pretend he is not there. It might as well be a law of nature that food and drink should appear at the table of their own accord for all the attention the waiter draws to himself. It is only when the miracle of dining does not go as planned that you really notice him.

Why do we think this way? Why does the waiter do his best not to be overly noticed, and why do we do our best not to notice him too much— especially when it comes time to consider the tip? More than this, why does the dining experience go this way at all? You sit down, you order drinks, you mull over the menu, you order, you sit for an extended period of time, the waiter brings your food, you eat, he asks if you want dessert, you say no, he brings the check, your eyes bulge at the price, you mull over how much of a tip you should leave, you decide on an amount, your wife tells you to leave more, you leave more, the waiter whisks your payment away, he returns with receipt and mints, and after sitting a few minutes more you

15. Lewis, *Miracles*, 305
16. Chesterton, *Napoleon of Notting Hill*, 312

finally leave. Probably most of us would describe our dining experience in this way. We could look forward to 90 percent of all dining experiences in the future going exactly like this. What's strange about it is that though it is predicable, there is no natural law of the restaurant, there is only the magic of dining.

The universe is very much like this. We partake of life every day. We sit down at its table and expect the courses to come as they should. But to assume they will come is not the same as saying they must come. That is because the one providing our meal is not our paid servant. He is not a hired hand. His is the waiter, yes, but he is also the chef, the butcher, the farmer, our host, and the one who brought us to table. He is all these things. None of it happens because it must. It happens because the one providing the meal wants it to.

There is nothing as ordinary as eating a meal, and there is nothing as ordinary as life. But the regularity of our experience does not mean such things must happen. No matter what it is, even the effects of gravity, are not guaranteed. When we drop a pen gravity does pull it down, and scientists can calculate the acceleration of that object. Scientists can even determine that gravity is the warping of space-time and be perfectly accurate in that conclusion. But at the same time when we drop the pen it is God pulling it down. He could cause the pen to float away, and in some places he does just that—ask the astronauts. But most of the time he does not do this to us. Why? Why does he do what we think is common or mundane?

I believe Chesterton touched on the truth when he said, "Perhaps God is strong enough to exult in monotony."[17] Perhaps God turns the world every day and is saying to us, "Look how cool that is!" Perhaps he causes the pen to fall to the ground just so we can remember the childhood song, "Head, and Shoulders, Knees, and Toes." Perhaps he causes the rain to fall on a place no man has ever visited just to chuckle at the foolishness of some men who suggest that unless a thing is measured by man it does not exist.

This is what Paul is talking about when he says God's invisible attributes are readily visible in the world around us. It is an active thing. It is a present thing, and not merely an echo of the Creator's voice from when the world was born. Paul's criticism of men in Romans 1 is that they twisted the truth of God into the lie, for this reason his wrath is revealed against all ungodliness. This is happening now; it is not just something in the future. The wrath of God is present even as the invisible attributes of God are present

17. Chesterton, *Orthodoxy*, 263

now. This is because men did not recognize God at work. How often do we do the same? How often do we only look for God in the extraordinary instead of in the ordinary?

Certainly God can act in unexpected ways. I have not been denying this. But when we only look and pray for God to act in an unexpected way as a sign of his working we are, in a sense, not really understanding who he is. When something quirky or surprising or downright amazing happens we are quick to call it God acting—and certainly it is that. But the fact that we are constantly looking for these things, or praising them as if at last God has done something praiseworthy, is to reveal the true nature of our hearts just as much as it reveals the foundation of what we think about deity. For really we should, at every moment, be pointing out that God is acting. When the wind rustles the trees we should exclaim, "Oh, God! What a refreshing breath of wind and a beautiful sound you are making in the trees!" When the sun shines down upon us we should sing praises saying, "God, thank you for bringing the sun again!"

Even when life is not going the way we want, our response should be to recognize God's hand at work. When there is sickness or trouble we should pray for healing and relief. At the same time we must not make the mistake of thinking God is far away. When he delays, when he does not act as quickly as we might like, and hope is fading and the troubles of this world have you downcast and unable to lift your head, then let me offer this advice. As you look down at your feet, unable to look at the blue sky, then really look at your feet. See how they stand upon the earth! Or, if you cannot stand consider how you sit in your chair or lay in the bed. Consider how you do not fly off into space, and know that God holds you there. Take a deep breath and realize He has filled your lungs. Listen to the pounding of your heart and realize he gives you every beat.

God is there. He is living and active. Ordinary things are only ordinary because we have gotten used to the regularity of the spectacular.

Now the point of all of this is to say we must have a proper understanding of divinity. If we are going to unravel the mystery of the triune God, then we must understand what it means for there to be deity at all. At the most basic level, this is what it means for there to be a God. He is not merely the giver of promises. He is not merely the Creator and Savior. He is the sustainer. He acts in extraordinarily ordinary ways, and if we say we know him, then we must give voice to this. With every breath we ought to say, "Ah! Thanks again, God!" With every bite of food and every swig of water we should lift our hearts and souls to glorify and thank him. We must look at the world around us and not get wrapped up in the *what* of what is going on. Rather, we must recognize *who* is always at work. For long before it was said, "Let there be light!" there was already the light of personality. And every time the light of the sun shines it is because that same personality says, "Do it again!"

2

Yahweh's Monotheism
and the Intolerance of Truth

"And that dismal cry rose slowly
And sank slowly through the air,
Full of spirit's melancholy
And eternity's despair!
And they heard the words it said—
Pan is dead—Great Pan is dead—
Pan, Pan is dead."

—Elizabeth Barrett Browning

The common reality shared among nearly all the ancient cultures was one filled with personality and power. They could all agree on this. It was as familiar to them as McDonalds, cell phones, and cars are to us. The trouble is that though clearly there is a God—a being of immense power and eternality—it does not follow that there is only one God or who this God is or what he wants. We are therefore drawn to the first distinguishing feature of the Christian God, that he is the only God.

Many people stumble at this point when trying to understand (or trying incredibly hard not to understand) the doctrine of the Trinity. They get wrapped up in the plurality of God and not his unity. But the very reason the doctrine is of a triune God and not a tri-theistic God (i.e. three gods) is because it is built on the truth of absolute monotheism. There is only one God and this God is Yahweh. His existence is the measure of all truth, whether science or morality, theology or philosophy. It is the foundation which cannot be abandoned if the doctrine of the Trinity is to be properly understood.

POLYTHEISM

Yahweh's monotheism was revealed in a world of polytheism. More often than not, the different gods were parts of creation that were deified in the eyes of men. This, of course, resulted in hundreds, and probably thousands of gods being created. Just one facet of creation could produce many different gods. In a study of Near Eastern storm-gods, Daniel Schwemer identified a dozen or so different gods all having something to do with this phenomenon of nature.[1] Where there were storm-gods, there were bound to be fertility gods, gods of the earth, of the sky, and of various other things. Naturally if you have all these different gods they would form a community of sorts and thus polytheism was born.[2] From the time of the patriarchs to Christ, there were thousands of gods worshipped.

Each god or goddess had a particular part to play in the maintenance of the universe. The primary purpose of the gods was the maintaining of cosmic order by holding back chaos.[3] They did this in several ways, ranging from caring for individual families to making sure the celestial bodies moved the right way, or fighting creatures of chaos (usually creatures associated with the sea, such as leviathan[4]). While there could be and were fights between the gods and goddesses, generally speaking when the divine hierarchy was organized properly, then the world would function the way that it should.

Humans played a very important role in this work of maintaining the cosmos. The cult practices—prayers, incantations, burning of incense, offering of sacrifices and the like—played a part in sustaining the gods and helping to maintain order. According to Egyptologist Jan Assmann, "The

1. Schwemer, "Storm-Gods of the Ancient Near East," 121–68.

2. Walton, *Ancient Near Eastern Thought*, 104.

3. The Egyptian god Seth may be an exception to this. He seems to personify chaos. See Assmann *God and Gods*, 28–52.

4. An interesting point here is that in Genesis 1, God is said to have made all the great sea monsters. These are to be understood as creatures of chaos and the Bible is saying even these creatures were given their function by the one God.

meaning of cult and ritual in Egypt and in presumably all other primary religions, is to reconcile human society with the divine world, to integrate human life into the process and cycles of cosmic life . . . to maintain the cosmos by assisting the gods in overcoming chaos."[5] Think about that! This is not your ordinary idea of religion. This was not just going to church because, well, all Christians are expected to go to church. We are not talking about *faith* by which we mean some personal conviction that has little or no impact on the larger universe. After all, if we do not go to church for a week or a month we do not worry about whether the crops will grow, or if babies will be born, or generally that the world will fly apart at the seams. But this is *exactly* what might have happened in the perspective of those ancient peoples if men and women failed in their rituals. A curse might come upon the family, or your wife might be barren, your crops might fail, your city might come to ruin, or the sun itself might not shine. In other words, humans may have been created to serve the gods, but only because the gods themselves were supposed to be busy making sure chaos and darkness did not overrun the world. By serving the gods—not just one, but all of them in one way or another—human beings could join in the effort of holding back the encroaching night.

This worldview was shared by many Near Eastern cultures, and was especially true of those cultures ancient Israel interacted with. It was even true for the culture the Christian Church found itself in after it spread out from Jerusalem. When the Roman Empire began to collapse, one of the perceived causes was the fact that so many people were abandoning the gods of the Empire for the one God of Christianity. Rome was falling because the Roman gods were being forsaken. These gods would not or could not maintain the order the Empire had given the world. If you think this is so strange an idea, then just consider how many American Christians are saying that America is in the state she is in because she has abandoned God. The main difference between them may be that the pagans had a more fatalistic and hopeless perspective. They could not cling to the idea that the gods had some master plan, some grand purpose for the world. Instead, the success of the gods' work was never assumed, and might fail at any time. Order in the cosmos was only as strong as the weakest link in the order of life, in this case, mankind.[6]

5. Assmann, *Akhenaten to Moses*, 8.
6. Assmann, *God and Gods*, 17–18.

Participation by all of the gods and man was important in this grand task. This is why polytheism could exist as a system. No one god was jealous of worship. There could be different gods in the same town, in the same house, even in the same temple. As long as a god's needs were being met, he did not feel his position was threatened if other gods were worshiped as well.[7] If Zeus remained king of Olympus he did not begrudge Apollo, Athena, or Aphrodite sacrifice and worship. No one god did everything, so while Zeus might have been the thunder-god and king of Olympus, he was not the god of love and fertility, or of healing or death. The same was true in Egypt; Amun might be considered the chief god, but it was Osiris who was god of the underworld, and Horus was god of kingship.[8] There were all sorts of powers at work in the world so it was only natural that there should be just as many gods, each important in his or her way.

Naturally the different cultures of the world would identify gods with common ideas or phenomenon. I mentioned earlier there being dozens of storm-gods in the Near East, but there were also fertility gods, gods of war, gods of the sky, the earth, and nearly anything else you can think of. There were really no false gods, and as a result there could be no false beliefs.[9] This was the great achievement of polytheism. Cultures could interact and relate to one another because their system was a tolerant one. Not only could a person go from one town to another without his beliefs being dismissed as false, but kingdoms could make meaningful treaties with one another because of the acceptance of other gods, or the ability to equate gods with one another. Whenever two nations entered into a treaty they would usually call upon the gods to enact and maintain that treaty. To better accomplish this, it was desirable that the gods being called upon be roughly equal in status and function, even if they had different names in the different cultures. Had the Greeks and the Norse people ever entered into treaty, it is possible Zeus and Thor would have been called upon to ensure the treaty. Both were gods of thunder, and so must be roughly equivalent to one another.

The Greeks were very good at this sort of translation of gods. I don't mean the translation of their names, but rather of the gods themselves. The ancient historian Herodotus provides an example of this when he equated the Egyptian god Amun with the Greek Zeus.[10] The Greeks even did this

7. Walton, *Ancient Near Eastern Thought*, 112.

8. Wilkinson, *Complete Gods and Goddesses*, 119–20, 200–1.

9. Walton, *Ancient Near Eastern Thought*, 111.

10. Herodotus, *Histories*, 109.

with the God of the Bible, identifying Yahweh as Iao, the god of time who appeared as "Hades in winter, Zeus in springtime, Helios in summer, and Habros Iao in autumn."[11]

The nature of treaties in the ancient world meant that the parties involved would find their religions being drawn into closer connection.[12] There would be an intermingling of traditions, practices, and names. Indeed, by the second century AD Plutarch could write, "Nor do we think of the gods as different gods among different peoples…but just as the sun and moon and the heavens and earth and the sea are common to all, but are called by different names by different peoples," so too the gods are called by different names but are the same gods.[13] So, in a sense, there were not multiple religions in the ancient world. There was only one, though different cultures applied different names and practiced different rites. This is what is so remarkable about polytheism. It allowed for the translatability of gods and traditions, producing a great deal of tolerance that can be expressed this way: you have your gods, I have mine, and in the end they're all the same.

If this sounds eerily similar to the type of relativism that we see today, then you are not far wrong. There was a great deal of liberality and tolerance in the polytheistic system because no one had a claim to *the* truth. Certainly there was truth, and in a sense all the different traditions had some small bit of it. The point, though, is that no one really had all of it, even though everyone was looking for it. This is what allowed there to be all sorts of different gods and practices during the time period when great empires absorbed many smaller nations with their own unique practices. It is why Alexander, when he conquered Egypt, did not tear down the Egyptian temples, but rather incorporated himself into their system.

Within polytheism it is good and proper that all sorts of different gods be worshiped. What would be evil would be the insistence on there being only one God. For if all the other gods were neglected then they would grow weaker and so be unable to do their part in maintaining order.[14] This is what made the monotheism of the Israelites so radical and so despised. It was not just that they were different, but that in their difference they

---

11. Assmann, *God and Gods,* 55.

12. Magnetti, "Function of the Oath," 825. See also Assmann, *God and Gods,* 55.

13. Plutarch, *Isis and Osiris,* 9.

14. Assmann, *God and Gods,* 47.

claimed to know the only true God, and to possess the only truth. In so doing they threatened the entire world.

YAHWEH'S MONOTHEISM

The God revealed in the scriptures leaves no room for doubting his claim to be the only God. Just consider Isaiah 45:18–25.

> For thus says the LORD,
> Who created the heavens,
> Who is God,
> Who formed the earth and made it,
> Who has established it,
> Who did not create it in vain,
> Who formed it to be inhabited:
> I am the LORD, and there is no other.
> I have not spoken in secret,
> In a dark place of the earth;
> I did not say to the seed of Jacob,
> 'Seek Me in vain';
> I, the LORD, speak righteousness,
> I declare things that are right.
> Assemble yourselves and come;
> Draw near together,
> You who have escaped from the nations.
> They have no knowledge,
> Who carry the wood of their carved image,
> And pray to a god that cannot save.
> Tell and bring forth your case;
> Yes, let them take counsel together.
> Who has declared this from ancient time?
> Who has told it from that time?
> Have not I, the LORD?
> And there is no other God besides Me,
> A just God and a Savior;
> There is none besides Me.
> Look to Me, and be saved,
> All you ends of the earth!
> For I am God, and there is no other.
> I have sworn by Myself;
> The word has gone out of My mouth in righteousness,
> And shall not return,

That to Me every knee shall bow,
Every tongue shall take an oath,
He shall say,
"Surely in the LORD I have righteousness and strength.
To Him men shall come,
And all shall be ashamed who are incensed against Him.
In the LORD all the descendants of Israel
Shall be justified, and shall glory.

Right at the beginning of this passage there is a clear declaration of who this God is: the LORD. This is the way most English translations render the divine name, and it muddles things a bit, because of course, neither *God* nor *Lord* is a proper name. It is like a designation of office, like *king* or *president*. Had Isaiah really used the terms for *Lord* or *God,* then there would have been some confusion about exactly who was claiming to be the only God. But the prophet is very particular in who this God is. Isaiah writes, "For thus says the LORD." This word, where every letter is capitalized, is an indicator of the divine name: Yahweh.

This name is very specific, and it does not denote a general idea or some force of nature. The ancient Egyptians under the heretic pharaoh, Akhenaton, flirted with monotheism for a brief period. Akhenaton claimed there was only one God: Aten, who was identified with the solar disk."[15] The God of Abraham, Isaac, and Jacob was not identified with some symbol or physical representation. He was to be known by his deeds, his law, and his name: *Ahey Ashur Ahey*—I Am That I Am is how it is traditionally rendered in English, though it could be I Am Who I Am. This is shortened to merely I Am[16], which becomes the name known to all generations: Yahweh. According to Hill and Walton, the name "connotes the personal, eternal, and all-sufficient aspects of God's nature and character."[17] Contained within his name is the absolute perfect description of who and what he is: the absolute being who is dependent on no one and yet is absolutely and perfectly personal enough to make such a claim with a straight face. It is no joke. It is not hyperbole. His name is not a force of nature or experience of the universe. It is a name which lays claim to existence and life not as a gift bestowed or stolen, but as being always only the bearer's. *Yahweh,* because no other name will do.

15. Wilkinson, *Complete Gods and Goddesses,* 236–241.
16. Exod 3:14
17. Hill and Walton, *Survey of the Old Testament,* 113.

At the same time this name identifies its owner as the absolutely unique one, it also is the name associated with a specific covenant given to a specific people. Not only is this one self-existent and the creator of heaven and earth, but he has given this name to call to mind the promise made to Abraham, Isaac, and Jacob. It was this name, *Yahweh*, which Moses was to declare to the people: the name of the one who was to set them free. It is the name which introduces the Ten Commandments, for God says, "I am Yahweh your God, who brought you out of the land of Egypt, out of the house of bondage."[18] It is the name of the God who not only freed the people of Israel but made them a special possession, giving them laws, and who dwelt between the cherubim of the ark.

This is the same God who is identified in Isaiah 45. He is the God of the Israelites and lays claim to have created the heavens and the earth. The ancient world would not have been overly upset by this. After all, each nation had its own deities and it was no surprise that a nation's supreme deity (or at least one of the higher deities) would be named as being the creator of everything. But then Yahweh says something startling. He says, "I am Yahweh, and there is none else." Several times, in fact, this claim is made in Isaiah 45 and it is important not to miss the significance. Yahweh is saying that he, not Amun, not Zeus, not Marduk, not Ba'al, not any other god you can think of is truly God. This is not a type of henotheism where one god is elevated above the rest. No, Yahweh says, "There is no other God besides Me," and again, "For I am God, and there is no other."

What a radical statement! What a completely intolerant claim! There is no other? Certainly some gods were elevated above others. The Assyrians went to war in the name of their god Assur, elevating him above the gods of the conquered people for the sake of order.[19] They at least had the decency to say the gods were real enough to be destroyed, but this God, he does not even do that! Yahweh says there is no other God. He makes it even more explicit in Isaiah 44:6 where he says, "I am the First and the Last; besides Me there is no God."

Yahweh does not seek to destroy other gods; he treats them as nothing, and commands his people to view them as nothing. This is why the Bible talks so much about idolatry. If there is only one God, then any other gods are mere creations of men. There is no power in them, the only mark of their existence, the only power in them, is the power of wood, stone or

---

18. Exod 20:2 and Deut 5:6
19. Dise, *Empires Before Alexander*, 91.

metal, the power to be cut, broken, or burned, or to be used as some bit of furniture. Those who serve such things are acting foolishly and abominably. This can be seen in Isaiah 45:20–21, where God mocks those who carry around their idol, praying to a god who cannot save them. Yahweh calls on the gods to work together—which polytheists thought could happen. The gods could enter into counsel, even as the gods of Olympus gathered to discuss the Trojan War. Yahweh says, Go ahead, put your heads together, let all the wisdom and might of the all the pantheons of the world come together and tell what things will come to pass. He calls on the gods to tell what happened in the past and what the end of those events will be.[20] What historian would not love to be able to do that? Every historian acknowledges that there are things he does not know about the past, and few would dare predict the future based on past results. Yet historians are mere men. Certainly the gods should be able to do such a thing. But even the gods cannot always tell where a thing will end. What is Yahweh's point? That he alone has this ability because he alone is God.

His ability to know the past and foresee the future is not because he has some crystal ball, or is really good at probabilities. Yahweh's ability to tell what is going to happen stems from the fact that he causes it to happen. As he says in Isaiah 44:24–26, "Thus says the LORD, your Redeemer, and the one who formed you from the womb, I, the LORD, am the maker of all things, stretching out the heavens by Myself and spreading out the earth all alone, causing the omens of boasters to fail, making fools out of diviners, causing wise men to draw back and turning their knowledge into foolishness, confirming the word of his servant and performing the purpose of his messengers." The thrust of this passage is that it is God who acts to bring these things about. He declares it and then does it. "He does according to His will in the army of heaven and among the inhabitants of the earth. No one can restrain His hand or say to him, 'What have You done?'"[21]

It is for this reason that Yahweh can say there is no other Savior. Salvation from calamity can come from no one else but him, because he is the only one who acts. In fact, he calls on the gods to do anything, to do good or evil so that it might be known. Do something! He tells them. A few chapters later in Isaiah, Yahweh dismisses them and says, "I bring peace and create

20. Isa 41:21–24.
21. Dan 4:35.

calamity."[22] In other words, he brings a blessing or a curse, good or evil. Who can save from his hand? Only he can.

As Christians we too often forget this. We get nervous about saying that bad things happen because God causes them. Usually we resort to saying that God *allows* certain things to happen. This makes us feel better, safer. But it is not safe at all. Because if calamity is out of God's control, how will he ever stop it? How will he ever turn it for his purposes? This principle was at work when God brought Nebuchadnezzar and the Babylonians—an idolatrous people—to punish Judah. What greater calamity could there be but the destruction of the temple, the sacking of the holy city, and the enslavement of the chosen people of God? While breaking down walls, while killing, and feasting on the spoils of victory, the Babylonians would have been making thank offerings to their gods. While enslaving the people of Judah, they would have been taunting them, saying how their gods were mightier than the Israelite God. But all the while Yahweh was telling his people that this calamity came about because *he* caused it.

So just look at what has been done in these few verses of Isaiah! All the pantheons are cast down. They are not treated reverently as the symbols of advanced and tolerant civilizations. These gods are nothing. It is not that Yahweh has defeated them, but that they were never there to be defeated. Those who worship them are fools—just as foolish as the one who says in his heart there is no God.

What is being claimed is nothing less than absolute truth. There is no room for variance, no room for one culture to have gods and traditions while Israel had another God with other traditions. There could be no shared worldview so long as there were separate deities because Yahweh was not and is not claiming to merely be Israel's God. He calls all the people of the earth to himself, saying, "Turn to Me and be saved, all the ends of the earth; for I am God and there is no other." This is not a passive call, for he says, "I have sworn by Myself, the word has gone forth from My mouth in righteousness and will not turn back, that to Me every knee will bow, and every tongue swear allegiance." Like it or not, this God will bring all the peoples of earth to his feet, and they will acknowledge that he alone is God, and he alone is the measure of truth.

This is something dramatic, something completely intolerant. I do not mean on the part of Isaiah or the people of Israel. This is intolerant on God's part. Amun, Marduk, or Zeus would allow people to worship other gods.

22. Isa 45:7.

They accepted this. Amun was fine if people worshipped Horus so long as Amun did not lose his place. The same would be true with every other god—except Yahweh. He says that everyone will swear allegiance to him and him alone.

All of this is bad enough for polytheists. To say their gods are nothing and never were anything strikes at the very heart of their idea of how the world works. All the rituals, all the sacrifices, the participation of the human with the divine in the world of maintaining the cosmos is not really taking place. But what is really hard to swallow, is that Yahweh is not merely specific in who he is, but also in what he expects. Consider Isaiah 45:25 which says, "In the LORD all the offspring of Israel will be justified and will glory." Now it's easy to think that *justified* has something to do with salvation, but I do not think that is what is going on here. I think this word would be better rendered as *vindicated*. It is not so much getting the accounts balanced with God, but with being proven right to the world.

Why would Israel need to be vindicated? The first answer is that they believed in only the one true God. A more complete answer would take into consideration that this Yahweh is the God of the covenant—a covenant of promises and of commandments. These commandments were not designed to save, but to show God's requirement for men, and to mark as peculiar those who obeyed them. They were not arbitrary, but tied to what Yahweh would or would not tolerate. Just consider Leviticus 18. It forbids several things, and many of them have to do with sexual conduct. Several things are mentioned: incest, adultery, homosexuality, bestiality, just to name a few. These things are forbidden because God despises them. God says, "Do not defile yourself with any of these things; for by these the nations are defiled, which I am casting out before you."[23] This shows that Yahweh's moral law is being applied to all nations, and not just to Israel. He gave the land to Israel not because they were worthy of it, but because he was punishing those nations which inhabited it before the Israelites. Yahweh had done nothing less than decide what is right and what is wrong, enforcing his will on a people who did not worship him. This is utterly intolerant and rejects the polytheistic system that might be summarized as different strokes for different folks. Yahweh rejected this, and said the way he provides is the only way. His truth is the only truth.

23. Lev 18:24.

IMPLICATIONS

I have used the word *intolerant* to describe monotheism, and I think that this fits well with the reality of the revelation. Many people do not like this word because it conjures up images of unkindness and evil, but this is not what I mean. What I mean is the kind of intolerance that correct math shows to incorrect math. It is the intolerance of reality.

Yahweh makes a claim against all gods and against all worldview systems. His claim is absolute and unyielding. It is not merely a claim to existence, but a claim that because of his existence, he gets to choose what is right and what is wrong. He has the right to declare what is acceptable human behavior and what is abominable in his sight. Recognizing Yahweh's claim to be the only God is not merely to acknowledge his existence like one might acknowledge the existence of a cat. Rather, to hold to this monotheism is to orient one's entire life to align with the truth of who this God is and what he declares. This monotheism lays claim to more than religious service and demands a particular lifestyle.

The intolerance of truth is two-sided. Upon the one hand you have our natural inclinations, the morality determined by human experience and preference. At its core is the individual and collective declaration of, My way! And my way only! On the other hand you have the voice of the God of Abraham, Isaac, and Jacob claiming to be the wellspring of truth and life, claiming to be the only true God. Neither side is willing to back down. This is how it has been since Adam sinned. Those who, by God's grace, had their hearts softened and their wills changed, found themselves at odds with their fellow men. Those ancient Israelites who were faithful to the Torah of Yahweh found themselves in conflict with their countrymen: rather like Elijah found himself set against King Ahab and Queen Jezebel. Or perhaps it is like Isaiah proclaiming woe to Israel. Then again it might be like the Christians being told they must give up their sacred texts and burn incense to Caesar.

Today we face the same trouble. The world has decided that what Yahweh declared perverse is actually good, wholesome, and healthy. Churches are troubled when the command of Yahweh to gather comes into conflict with pandemic lockdowns. What are churches that meet but uncaring, unloving, and ignorant? At least, that is what the world will say. A similar accusation must have been leveled against the ancient Israelites and ancient Christians who refused to do good for the society by burning incense to Caesar and worshiping the imperial gods. The difference, some would say, is that we know that the gods are not real, but science is true. This only serves to illustrate the point. Science is just as real to us as the gods were to the ancient peoples. Those who appeal to the authority of science do not get to assume authority over the commands of Yahweh, any more than the priests of Ba'al got to assume authority over the people of God. He is far too intolerant of that; for every authority that sets itself against his ways sets itself up as another god. This Yahweh will not tolerate, though that authority be a king, a president, a governor, or mayor. He is Yahweh, and to him every knee will bow and every tongue swear allegiance.

3

The Holiness of Yahweh

"Are You not from everlasting, O LORD my God, my Holy One?"

—HABAKKUK 1:12

THE PROPHET HABAKKUK OFFERED a confused complaint. There was vio-
lence, wickedness, and injustice in his country and among his people. The
land of Judah was filled with lawlessness for the people had abandoned
the Torah of the one God, and the prophet was confused. The northern
kingdom of Israel had also been lawless and idolatrous, and Yahweh had
used the Assyrians to bring judgment. Lawlessness was continuing in the
southern kingdom, but the hammer of God was growing weak. Assyria's
power was diminished, and the covenant was broken and being broken by
Judah. Who, then, would punish Judah if Assyria was gone? Would lawlessness continue?[1]

God's answer to this was rather unexpected. He was going to bring the
Chaldeans—a violent people who worshipped false gods—in order to judge
Judah. Of course the prophet was astonished by this. "Are you not from
everlasting, O LORD my God, my Holy One?" he says. "You are of purer
eyes than to behold evil, and cannot look on wickedness. Why do you look
on those who deal treacherously, and hold Your tongue when the wicked
devours a person more righteous than he?"[2] In other words, God is holy,

1. Hill and Walton, *Survey of the Old Testament*, 662.
2. Hab 1:12, 13.

32

how could he use a people who were, quite frankly, worse than Judah in order to punish Judah? So Habakkuk is either trying to remind God of his own holiness, or else the prophet is trying to wrap his mind around what Yahweh is doing. He calls Yahweh "my Holy One." The NIV, ESV, NASB, and NKJV all say this, and it almost sounds like he is saying, "my dear" or "my darling" or "my love." Except in this case he says, "my Holy One."

My wife will call me "my love" and it is a very intimate, almost possessive phrase. It is not that she somehow owns me, but rather that I own her heart. In the same way Habakkuk's addressing God as "my Holy One" indicates that in the prophet's heart and soul, Yahweh is his holy one. Yahweh possesses Habakkuk's heart and soul in that way.

This really is a rather strange way to address God for Evangelicals. We tend to focus on God's love, saying things like he is the lover of my soul. Other times we might focus on his grace—his amazing grace. Other times, if we feel love and grace have been distorted, we'll shift to the wrath of God. But it is not love, or grace, or even wrath that defines God in Habakkuk's heart; it is, rather, holiness.

Now it is certainly true that the prophet makes this statement about God because the wicked Babylonians were about to punish Judah. That kind of contrast between holiness and wickedness was certainly on the forefront of his mind. But it is the fact that he calls Yahweh *my* holy one that I'd like to focus on. What does it mean? What does Habakkuk have in mind when he says this about God? What is this *holiness* that should spring to his mind? And why should he not have complained that God is love and so should not have punished Judah? Why holiness? What is so special about it?

I am convinced that if at once we acknowledge that Yahweh is the one, true, living God, then we must at the same time recognize his absolute holiness. We cannot get around it, for it is a logical necessity. It is God's holiness that is the defining aspect of his nature, and the part we must deal with—more than love, more than mercy, or grace, or wrath, more than his creatorship and sovereignty. Holiness is the sum of all these things and then some. This is what sprang to mind for Habakkuk, and it is the part of God we must come to terms with if we are truly to understand who he is and who we are. It is only by understanding Yahweh's holiness that we can comprehend how each person of the Trinity acts to glorify this holiness, to satisfy it, and wrap us in it. Only by letting him be the Holy One of our hearts can we truly appreciate and unravel the mystery of the Trinity.

DEFINING HOLINESS

Holy is one of those words used by Christians all the time but with little thought about what it means. It is so familiar to us, so much a part of the Christian vocabulary, that it is at once familiar and foreign. John Feinberg, in his book *No One Like Him*, says the idea that is most often associated with *holiness* is moral purity. By this he means, "God is free from the pollution of sin, for he cannot sin."[3] Then there is Wayne Grudem who, in his *Systematic Theology* says, "The idea of holiness . . . [includes] both separation from evil and devotion to God's own glory . . ."[4] Both of these theologians define holiness along moral lines, that God cannot sin or commit evil. For Grudem God is *separate* from evil, indicating he can only do what is good. His choice of words is interesting because this idea of separateness seems to be a more exact meaning of the word *holy*. As R.C. Sproul said:

> The primary meaning of *holy* is "separate." It comes from an ancient word that meant "to cut" or "to separate." To translate this basic meaning into contemporary language would be to use the phrase, "a cut apart." Perhaps even more accurate would be the phrase, "a cut above something."[5]

Sproul goes on to say that God's holiness is transcendence. He is high above everything and everyone.

The difference between moral purity and transcendence may seem irrelevant. Why is morality not sufficient? After all, it provides a reason for why God punishes sin. But God is not the judge of humanity and punisher of sin because he is some kind of divine superhero fighting for truth, justice, and the American way. It is not that he is bound by the idea that with great power comes great responsibility. That was Spider-Man's creed, a burden placed upon him when he received his powers. But no one gave God his powers. No one gave him the throne of heaven. No one gave God omnipotence, omniscience, and omnipresence. God is not obligated to do moral things as if some law has a demand on his services. There is no outside measure of right and wrong. There is no one who has directed him or has given him instruction or taught him Justice.[6] There is no law which can

---

3. Feinberg, *No One Like Him*, 342.
4. Grudem, *Systematic Theology*, 202.
5. Sproul, *Holiness of God*, 29.
6. Isa 40:14.

hold him accountable, except the law of his word. This is why we must be careful in defining *holiness* with morality in mind.

God does not act justly according to some outside moral code. This is something which is very difficult for us Christians to understand and accept, but it is the lesson of the book of Job. There we are told both by the opening narrative and by God himself that the man Job was righteous. Sometimes people read that and they begin to equivocate. They point out that the scriptures say there is none righteous, no not one. So Job's suffering was really deserved. But what is interesting about this argument is that it is the very one made by Job's friends—one for which they were rebuked in the end. No, Job was righteous, sufficiently righteous to make the point of the book. When God appears at the end he does not go into a gospel presentation. He does not enter into a discussion about how Job really is a sinner deserving of loss and suffering. No, God's response was to blast Job with questions. He overwhelms Job with his awesome power, majesty, wisdom, and his complete otherness; in other words, he overwhelms the man with his absolute holiness. And what was Job's response? He says, "I have heard of You by the hearing of the ear, but now my eyes have seen You. Therefore I abhor myself and repent in dust and ashes."[7]

By all human standards of morality Job should not have suffered, for he had done nothing wrong. If anything, he had done everything right. God should have had no reason to inflict suffering. But God's answer was yes, Job was righteous, but it was also that God could not be put into any moral box. His wisdom is high above any man's, and there is no one who can bring him to court to give an account. Does this then mean that God is amoral? Not at all! What it does mean is that any concept of morality, of good and evil, is bound up in *who* God is. It is bound up in his "majestic holiness" not because he is a police officer enforcing an outside law, but because any sin, any good or evil, is bound up in how one relates to God.[8]

Part of the difficulty in communicating this concept of holiness is that it really needs to be experienced in order to be understood. It is like the idea of *beauty*. We can define beauty as something attractive or pleasing to the senses. But it is only when you see it or experience it that we know what beauty really is: like seeing a sunset on a night with just the right cloudiness, or the sound of water streaming over rocks. Holiness is like this, except it is even more elusive because we are so very unholy ourselves. Part of us

7. Job 42:5–6
8 Exod 15:11.

shrinks back from the holy, despising it, and to truly come face-to-face with holiness would be disastrous for us.

One way we can get a glimpse of holiness is through the record of other peoples' experiences of it. The Bible provides several such examples, and we have already considered Job, though he doesn't say directly that he experienced holiness. So we will look at a few other texts, and while doing so be sure to do two things. First, notice that there is a part of holiness that does have to do with morality, but it is always in man's relationship to God and not to some outside moral code. Second, try to feel what is being presented. The stories in scripture are meant to give us an experience just as much as they relay information. I mean that the narrative and descriptions are designed to get us into the story itself. The scriptures paint pictures just as much as they provide instructions.

The first passage we will examine is Leviticus 10:1–3.

> Then Nadab and Abihu, the sons of Aaron, each took his censer and put fire in it, put incense on it, and offered profane fire before the LORD, which he had not commanded them. So fire went out from the LORD and devoured them, and they died before the LORD. And Moses said to Aaron, "This is what the LORD spoke, saying: 'By those who come near Me I must be regarded as holy; and before all the people I must be glorified.'"

This little story takes place in between the consecration of the priesthood and laws concerning clean and unclean foods. It is sudden and dramatic. Nadab and Abihu, the sons of Aaron, offered strange or profane fire before Yahweh. We are not told what made it strange or profane. We are not even told what command had been broken, though it is likely they had transgressed the command of Exodus 30:9 which says, "You shall not offer strange incense on it,"—speaking of the alter of incense. It could also have been a reference to Exodus 30:34–38 which gives specific instructions on making incense, and perhaps the sons of Aaron had made impure incense.

Regardless of what made the fire profane, it is highly probable that Nadab and Abihu were drunk when it occurred. This can be inferred by what follows almost immediately in Leviticus 10:8–10. It is written that Yahweh spoke to Aaron (and it is interesting that he speaks directly to Aaron and not through Moses) instructing him and his sons not to drink alcohol when they go into the tabernacle lest they die. This warning is important because Aaron's two sons did die. They died suddenly and gruesomely. They had come with their censors full to the place where Yahweh was to meet them.

They had come perhaps not even knowing or comprehending what they were doing. Still, it was not as though they had killed anyone. They were not going into the tabernacle to steal articles of gold. They were not sneaking in with prostitutes into the Holy of Holies. They had merely had a different colored fire burning in their little bowls. Perhaps we could equate it with playing an organ instead of a piano for church music. That's what it might have seemed like to us, but not to God.

Did the men have time to scream as fire shot out from the presence of Yahweh and consumed them? Moses and Aaron watched in terror, perhaps trying to bat out the flames, but I imagine that the fire was so hot, so intense, and so surprising that by the time they realized something was wrong it was too late. There was no saving Nadab and Abihu. At some point Aaron must have cried out, "My sons! My sons! Why?" Then Moses turned to him—perhaps his voice was quivering in fear, or his voice had become firm, or maybe even he whispered in sudden realization—and said to Aaron, "This is what Yahweh spoke, saying, 'By those who come near Me I must be regarded as holy, and before all the people I must be glorified.'"

The NASB has a note that God might have said, "I will show Myself as holy," instead of "I must be regarded as holy." Not being a Hebrew scholar I cannot be certain which it should be, but both seem to convey what happened. Yahweh had showed himself to be holy. At the same time Nadab and Abihu had not regarded Yahweh as holy in that they approached his tabernacle drunk and not with the proper fire. It did not even cross their mind.

But it was on God's mind.

It is always on God's mind. What is remarkable in this instance is just what has been stated before: there was no clear command that was broken. Of the two passages that might be in view, only Exodus 30:34–38 offers a punishment for the transgression. The command was that the one who transgressed was to be cut off from his people. Did this mean death? As far as I can tell it is possible that yes it meant death, but it might just as well have meant banishment from the community and covenant of promise. But Exodus 30 indicates that *people* were to enact the punishment. In the Leviticus passage, *God* gives out the punishment. So I am inclined to think that what occurred was not really about either command in Exodus being transgressed. There was a different emphasis. It was that there was a blatant and unacceptable infringement upon the holiness of Yahweh. I do not think that God spoke quickly and quietly to Moses as the bodies lay smoking on the floor of the tabernacle. Leviticus 10:3 reads almost as though Moses is calling something to mind. He is saying, perhaps in a trance or a whisper, "This is what Yahweh meant when he said . . ." Again, Moses is not quoting some part of Exodus or Leviticus, but it is almost like something else. It is something that perhaps Moses does not quote word for word, but it is certainly present throughout the entire law. It is the kind of thing that is present in Exodus 19:22 where Yahweh said, "Also let the priests who come near the LORD consecrate themselves, lest the LORD break out against them." Or again, a few verses later in Exodus, "Do not let the priests and the people break through to come up to the LORD lest he break out against them."[9]

There is something reserved for God, something special about being in his presence that is above and beyond the law. It is not moral in the sense that we are used to. Usually when we talk about sin a connection is made to hurting people, almost as if this was the primary reason sin is bad. But as you consider the deaths of Nadab and Abihu, ask yourself this: what humans were being hurt by these two men? All they did was offer fire, and so far as we can tell, the only two people who saw it were Moses and Aaron. The people were perhaps watching from a distance, but surely even if they were all gathered, only the front row would have caught a glimpse of the fire in the men's bowls. So it was not an offense against the sensibilities of the people. It harmed none of them, but it was an offense against the holiness of Yahweh.

Something very similar is recorded in 1 Samuel 6 when the Philistines sent the Ark of the Covenant back into Israel. The ark arrived at Beth Shemesh and the people were so happy they offered sacrifices to Yahweh. Think of it! They were filled with such excitement that this sign and symbol of their God had returned that they were giving him sacrifice. They were happy for themselves and for him! But their joy turned to horror when the text says 50,070 people were struck by Yahweh. It is possible that the original number was only seventy and that a scribal error increased it to such a large number, but the point is that many people died. Why? Because they had dared look inside the ark.[10] Again, they had not hurt anyone, but the men of Beth Shemesh knew what the cause of their suffering was. They said, "Who is able to stand before this holy LORD God?"[11] They did not say, "Silly people! Don't you know that you broke this law or that, and you

9. Exod 19:24
10. 1 Sam. 6:19
11. 1 Sam.6:20

38

really hurt the citizens of Beth Shemesh?" No, they focused on the holiness of God, the holiness they had offended.

Then there was the incident when David was trying to move the ark to Jerusalem. There was a great procession, with music and dancing. It was like a grand parade moving through the land with the ultimate destination being the capital city. The ark was not just a gold-covered box. It was the symbol of Yahweh's presence. Recall with what great horror Eli greeted the news that the ark had been lost. He took the news that his sons were dead with a stiff upper lip, but when told the ark was lost he fell back in his chair and died of a broken neck. There was a sense that God's favor was never quite what it should have been since the ark was lost, and now David was bringing it back! And it was in this atmosphere of jubilation that something dreadful happened. The cart carrying the ark tipped and a man—wanting to keep the ark from crashing to the ground—reached out and steadied the ark. We might draw a parallel to someone keeping a flag from falling to the ground. But God did not see this as a righteous or patriotic act. When Uzzah touched the ark we are told that the anger of Yahweh was roused against him, and God struck Uzzah dead.

As you can probably imagine, the sudden death of this man put a damper on the celebration. Everything ground to a halt. David was furious and afraid. Perhaps he was upset that the procession had stopped, and perhaps he was angry at himself for failing to follow the law concerning moving the ark. Then he was fearful for what might happen next. So he left the ark at the house of Obed-Edom. When at last David discovered God was no longer angry, he was finally able to bring the ark to Jerusalem. This time there was a difference. 2 Samuel 6:13 says it almost in passing, but it was central to the success of this second attempt. It says, "those bearing the ark . . ." The difference this time was that there was no ox cart. The ark was transported the way God commanded in the Torah. Failure to do this had been the original error. Uzzah had merely touched a gold-covered box, but this was not just any box. It was God's box. It was his possession, and he had commanded certain things about it when human beings played with it. Truly, though, it was not about the thing, not about the box or the incense. It was about God and the way men thought about God and treated him.

The three stories that have been examined should make us wonder what exactly holiness is, because none of these describes a situation where one human harmed another. The only people who were harmed were those whom God harmed. So the standard being presented is not the libertarian one that says that whatever doesn't break my leg or pick my pocket is acceptable. The question then is, since no humans were hurt by the sin itself, was God hurt?

While I do not think that any real injury was caused to God, I do think this question gets closer to the heart of the issue. The sons of Aaron, the men of Beth Shemesh, and Uzzah had not harmed God in a physical or psychological sense. But I do think they offended him and his holiness.

Unfortunately, causing offense has become the most taboo thing in the world. Everyone is offended by everything these days. Quite frankly, most of the people who are offended simply need to grow up. It is interesting, though, to think about what it actually means when someone is offended. What is the basis of their feeling offended? Usually it is the person himself who is offended: what he thinks is good or bad, or what makes him feel good or bad. And this is the source of criticism. Which of us is so important that whatever offends us personally is now somehow the law for the entire universe? Obviously, when it is thought about this way, none of us has that power or that importance. None of us is the measure of all that is offensive or permissible. This does not mean the feeling of offense goes away. It still gnaws away at us, but we understand that offense is a part of interacting with other human beings. There is a certain amount of tolerance that must be maintained if any interaction is to take place. To a greater or lesser extent, every single one of us has to get over ourselves. [12]

The temptation is to take this same approach with God. Why can't he just get over himself a little? He is love, after all. He should be able to just forgive and move on for the sake of relationship. Actually, this was an issue raised early on in Christian history. Heretics like Marcion identified the God of the Hebrew Scriptures—who seems often to act in wrath for offended holiness—as ultimately an evil God. A good God should be loving and forgiving, the kind of God the New Testament talks about. He should be able to forgive sins with barely a blink just because he wants to. Interestingly this is the kind of god presented in Islam, for Allah forgives when he wants, requiring no payment for sin if he doesn't wish it.

This is the kind of deity we are tempted to love. We are tempted to want a God like this. He would be humanesque, and we could relate to him, or criticize him, and probably understand him. He would be much nearer

---

12. There is, of course, a balance between bearing some offenses and stopping others. The current cancel-culture fad is an indication that few people have actually thought about what it means to be offended, and what things are worth addressing. The violent reaction of some to offense show that deep down we think of ourselves as gods.

to us. But this is not the God who has been revealed. Yahweh is not a man, not given to man's opinions. He is not dismissive of one part of himself for the sake of another. He doesn't want one thing so badly that he is willing or able to compromise himself in another way. He is not tainted by such things because he is majestic in holiness, as Exodus 15:11 says. He is utterly and completely other, but it is a glorious otherness. It is holiness that *is* and not just a theological concept. It is the terrible holiness that shuts up men's mouths, which causes them to be completely undone, and causes men to cry out, "Go away from me, Lord!"

Isaiah gives us a glimpse of what this holiness is. While in the temple he saw the Lord—the one who is truly the King of Israel—sitting on a throne with the glory of his robe filling the temple. It is an awesome description, but surely inadequate to what Isaiah actually saw.

> In the year that King Uzziah died, I saw the Lord sitting on a throne, high and lifted up, and the train of His *robe* filled the temple. Above it stood seraphim; each one had six wings: with two he covered his face, with two he covered his feet, and with two he flew. And one cried to another and said: "Holy, holy, holy *is* the Lord of hosts; The whole earth *is* full of His glory!" And the posts of the door were shaken by the voice of him who cried out, and the house was filled with smoke. So I said: "Woe *is* me, for I am undone! Because I *am* a man of unclean lips, and I dwell in the midst of a people of unclean lips; for my eyes have seen the King, the Lord of hosts."

Try to picture this in your mind's eye. There are these terrifying creatures standing above the throne (perhaps analogous to the cherubim covering the ark) and notice what they cry. They do not cry, "Love, love, love!" They do not cry, "Wrath, wrath, wrath."[13] In words which were like thunderous trumpets they cried, "Holy, holy, holy is Yahweh of hosts, the whole earth is full of His glory!"

At the sound of this the very door frame shook—perhaps from the concussive force of the declaration, but it was probably something more. The doorframe was probably experiencing what Isaiah the man was experiencing. Far from being filled with joy, Isaiah cries out in terror and pronounces a curse upon himself. He cries, "Woe is me, for I am undone!" This doom which had come upon him, this shattering of his very being was caused by seeing this Holy One upon the throne.

13. Sproul, *Holiness of God,* 23.

This is not the reaction we would expect. Isaiah does not fall down to worship in reverent awe. He does not lift his voice in praise. When actually standing in the presence of the Holy God he is shaken to the very core of his being in a disastrous way. Terror overcame him because he understood who he was seeing and when he saw the One on the throne he also saw himself. Instead of Isaiah's imperfection being blotted out by brilliant light, it was made stark and real. He was a man of unclean lips, living among a people of unclean lips. He was a *sinner.*

Compare this to the account of Luke 5:1–11. It is a fairly straightforward miracle performed by Jesus. After teaching, he tells Simon to move the boat further out and cast his nets. Of course we know what happens next. There is a huge catch, so big that the boat begins to sink. While everyone else scrambles around trying to save the boat, Peter does something very strange. Instead of being excited, instead of thanking Jesus, he falls down at Jesus' knees and pleads with him saying, "Depart from me, for I am a sinful man, O Lord!"

What a strange statement! The situation should have been one of thankfulness and praise, but Peter asks Jesus to go away. Why? What had happened? It was not the fish or the weighing down of the boat. It was the sudden weighing down of Peter's soul because he had seen through the fog of finances and glimpsed who it was that had done this wonderful thing. This was none other than *the* Lord. It was the One who was absolutely holy, and instead of praising this Lord, Peter says, "Go away, I am a sinner!"

The wonder of holiness had different affects on different creatures. The seraphim certainly saw it and appreciated it. They lifted their voices to tell heaven and earth and to shake the very physical universe that they beheld Holy Yahweh and that his glory filled the world. I am convinced that these heavenly creatures were not robots. They were not mere images and voices. They were and are beings as real as you or me, and they were so overcome with the wonder of God's holiness that they had to say it, they had to proclaim it. They fell prey to the same tendency we humans have to point out the obvious because it needs to be said. We might say, "That's a beautiful sunrise," or "That was a good movie," or "That was good food." It is not some jabbering tendency on our part, but a need to express something that touches our soul. So too the seraphim had to declare the holiness of Yahweh when they experienced it.

Contrast this to the reaction of Job, Isaiah, and Peter. Each realized something important when they found themselves in God's presence. They had known before that they were sinners, but the reality of their depravity and failure came crashing down upon them with all the force and urgency that caused the seraphim to make their declaration. These men suddenly appreciated the contrast between themselves and Yahweh. It was not just a distinction between Creator and creation; it was the contrast of the sinful with the holy. The theologian Thomas Watson called "holiness" the sparkling jewel in God's crown and the name by which he is known.[14] If it is his name, then it is who he is. It is not merely a robe he puts on, but rather is *the* defining nature of his being. When Job, Isaiah, and Peter came face-to-face with this they were undone because of their own nature: that of sin.

DEFINING SIN

Sin is not merely doing wrong. It is not the flouting of some code of conduct by which men are to abide and which God has been given the task of defending. It is more personal than this. It is defiant conduct against the very measure of the Holy. Sin strikes at God, at his authority, at his rights, at his very being. Watson says that sin is nothing less than an attempt to un-god God.[15] It is no wonder, then, that God hates sin because it is not only unlike him, but it is completely against him. And do not be mistaken, God hates both the sin and the sinner.

This is a hard truth for some people. We like to divorce the sinner from the sin, but that is like trying to separate the dog from doggishness, or trying to separate dirt from dirtiness. We need look no further for confirmation of this than Peter. Recall his statement when the full realization of who Jesus was came rushing in upon him. It was not, "Go away from me, Lord, for there is sin living in me." He was not saying he was the helpless carrier of a sinful parasite. No, Peter said, "Depart from me, for I am a sinful man, O Lord!" This was a statement about his person, about who *he* was, not some third entity called sin. This was who he was, body and soul. When Ezekiel 18:20 says that the soul who sins must die it really is talking about the sinner's soul, the human soul. It is not saying that the sin must die. It is saying the sinner must die. This is because sin, like holiness, is not a cloak. It is a nature.

This sin nature, this sinful soul is not some helpless, innocent thing. It is a ravenous beast with slobbering jaws, seeking to devour itself and the

14. Watson, *Body of Divinity*, 59
15. Watson, *Body of Divinity*, 60.

world around it. A consideration of one's self in the perfect mirror of God's word can leave no doubt of this. In the light of his terrible holiness each lust, every lie, every outburst of unrighteous anger, every covetous thought, every questioning of God's competency stands in sharp relief. They stand out for what they are: an attempt to dethrone the Lord of heaven and earth. It is an attempt to cast him down, remove the robe of his glory, and crush him underfoot. This is what sin really is. It cannot and must not be put in soft focus.

We are God's enemies by nature. How could it be otherwise when we seek to un-god him? But we are not on an equal plane with him. We are not two equal armies or even two unequal armies on the field of battle. No, we are not so grand. You and I are bugs, contemptible creatures, spiders really. What do you do when you find a spider in your home? Perhaps as a child you liked playing with spiders, and would gladly have kept one around, maybe to hang out in the upper corner of your bedroom where it would be out of the way and harmless. But now, as an adult, what if you found the spider crawling around in your bed? The natural reaction is to cast the thing away, to get rid of it because it invaded your space.

Jonathan Edwards equated our situation with that of the spider. He said that we are being held above a flame.[16] I do not know about you, but I do not pick up spiders and hold them over fire. They are too disgusting for that. I do not want to touch them. I want to destroy them, crush them utterly for I do not want them in my house, let alone my bed! They offend me.

This is how God views you in your natural state. This is how he views me. You are the wretched spider skittering around in the house of God, spinning your webs, trying to overcome him and bring him down in order to consume him and make his house your own. And God holds you in contempt for this. He holds me in contempt for this.[17] Our just reward is the bottom of his shoe, but our offense is against an eternal God and so long as our souls exist it will continue this way. This is the reality that so many people fail to grasp. Some have this false notion that when people die they suddenly cease sinning. As a result, these people question the fairness of God's holy punishment for sin and demand to know why the punishment is everlasting. But why do we think that sinners become saints when they die? We are not temporary sinners. If unregenerate, this is our eternal state.

16. Edwards, "Sinners in the Hands of an Angry God," 15.
17. Edwards, "Sinners in the Hands of an Angry God," 19.

The soul that sins must die, says Yahweh. It cannot abide in the presence of the holy. Job, Isaiah, and Peter knew this. Do you? These three had come into the presence of God, but the bitter truth of the matter is that we are always in his presence. It is only that we fail to appreciate it. For does not the psalmist say, "Where can I go from Your Spirit, or where can I flee from Your presence?"[18] It was the immediate, visible presence of God which caused these men to be undone, but God is everywhere. Does not his hand sustain us? Is not the whole earth filled with his glory? Truly, we are in his presence, his foot is poised above our heads, and it is only mercy which holds it back. It is only his grace that gives us life each moment.

We have a false perspective of this grace. It makes us careless. This patience on God's part is taken for granted by us. We experience it every moment, every day, and we think it is just life in its normal course. Little do we comprehend how gracious he is! But his grace is not reckless and it is not unending for sinners. His holiness is too important and potent for that. We cannot read the words of God without becoming aware that his terrible wrath is coming, and when it comes it will be absolute. It will be terrible and incredibly personal. Consider Isaiah 63:3 where God says, "I have trodden the winepress alone, and from the peoples no one was with Me. For I have trodden them in My anger, and trampled them in my fury; their blood is sprinkled upon My garments, and I have stained all My robes." Then again there is Ezekiel 8:18 which says, "Therefore I will act in fury. My eye will not spare nor will I have pity; and though they cry in My ears with a loud voice, I will not hear them." Such things are about real people. It is not some theological concept of sin that spatters his robes. It is not the idea of sin that cries out. God does not stop his ears to sin. He stops his ears to sinners. He will not listen to their cries, though they fill the air with a pitiable noise; he will not pity them.

It is tempting to get hung up on this wrath and this judgement which are so terrible, so sure, and so absolute. But consider this. Does the punishment outdo the crime? Oh, if only we could comprehend the glory and majesty of God! If only we could grasp the reality of his holiness! This is why it is so very important to understand that God is at work all around us, giving us every breath and every heartbeat. If we can internalize and possess this knowledge, then I dare say we will be on the way to a proper fear of Yahweh, and an appreciation of his holiness. It will be a terror and fear

18. Ps 139:7

45

to be sure, but it will also be a wonder because deep down we know and see the glory of his holiness.

As I sit here in the park writing this, the wind is blowing and the leaves are rustling in the trees. The sun is shining and the birds are singing. It is a glorious day! It is given by the hand of the glorious God, the Holy God. And when I think of what I have done, how I have longed for wicked things, how my tongue has said things I should not have said, and how deep in my heart I have wanted my way above God's—when I think that at this picnic table I am in the presence of Yahweh—I shudder. I shudder and wonder why I yet live. It is not because I am incredibly mean to other people, for I am a fairly decent person according to human standards. But when I think of this God who gives life, this God who is high above all things and is wrapped in glory and is holiness itself, then I am filled with terrible wonder. Deep in my soul I whisper, "My Holy One, Yahweh, why do You not strike?"

WHAT WILL HE DO?

It is a fearful thing to fall into the hands of the living God because his hands are holy hands. His face, which looks down at us, is a holy face. His eyes which behold us are holy eyes. But we are in his hands and we cannot avoid it. We cannot close our eyes and think that if we cannot see him then he cannot see us. He is there. What will he do?

You might think this is the wrong question. You may think a more appropriate one would be, *what can I do*? But the truth is that there is nothing you can do. You are naked and empty before the only living God, the one who has created and defines all truth. There is no shadow you can wrap yourself in to hide your imperfection and your utter rebellion and enmity toward this beautiful, glorious, awesome God. The only comfort you can offer yourself is self-deception. You can say that you're really not that bad, and that this talk about the holiness of God is exaggerated.

So then we circle back to the last chapter. This is the truth of God. It is a necessity of his existence as the one and only God. The fact that we recoil from it means that there is something in us that does not like it. Is that something our own desire, or is it the Spirit of God? Because let me tell you this, the Spirit of God is not afraid of the holiness of God.

This is why the concept of holiness is so important in understanding the Trinity. The work of the members of the Godhead is focused on this thing. Whether it is the punishment of sin, the plan of redemption, the transaction of justice and grace, or the outpouring of the Holy Spirit, all of it focuses on this one truth: God is holy. This holiness does not defile itself in order to relate to the unholy. God is far, far too zealous for his holiness to allow for that. And that is the way it should be. If only we grasped just how awesome his holiness is, then we too would be zealous for it. We would strive with every fiber of our being to truly be the images of God, reflecting this holiness.

Alas for sin!

There are some who say that the church's problem—and really western culture's problem—is that we have lost our grip on the concept of sin. Actually, I think our problem is that we have lost hold of the idea of holiness. It is only when we understand the beauty and wonder of God's holiness that we can come to appreciate the horror, repulsiveness, and putrid reality that is sin. Only when we appreciate that the holiness of God is the measure of all goodness and beauty can we see that sin is evil and should be mortified.

Holiness, not sin, is the central idea of what happens in the gospel. It is the undeniable, beautiful, unwavering holiness of Yahweh that we have attacked and for which wrath is being poured out on the world. It was this cup of *holy* wrath which Christ drank. He cried in the garden, "Father, if it is possible, let this cup pass from Me; nevertheless, not as I will, but as You will."[19] The cup he spoke of was the cup of the wrath of God. As it is written in Isaiah, he was wounded for our transgressions, crushed for our iniquities, and the chastisement for our peace was upon him.[20] For he who knew no sin had become sin for us.[21] This One who understood perfectly and experienced perfectly the holiness of God, and loved it absolutely, became in the eyes of holiness as one who despised holiness. The Son of God took upon himself the judgement side of holiness: the full fury of wrath so that in that appointed time the Father did not see his beloved Son, but an object of sin. The Son did this, so that when the Father looks at us, he does not see an object of sin. He sees his own Son. Holiness is appeased and justified in the wounds of the Lamb of God.

It is for holiness that the Spirit of God has been sent by the Father and Son. The Spirit works in us to produce holiness, because we, being unholy, cannot make ourselves holy. It is only the true source of holiness that can ever transform us from enemies of God to children of God.

19. Matt 26:39.
20. Isa. 53:3.
21. 2 Cor. 5:21.

In our natural, sinful condition we are naked and empty and there is no place to hide. The wrath of the Holy One burns against us—each of us personally. As I mentioned before, sin is a very personal thing, and God hates those who sin. We should rejoice in this, for if God did not hate personally then he would not love personally. If God just hated the general idea of sin, then he would only love the general idea of those who are in Christ. But the apostle Paul makes it clear in Galatians 2:20 that the love of God *is* personal when he says, "The life which I now live in the flesh I live by faith in the Son of God, who loved me and gave Himself for me." Do you understand how personal this love is? It is only natural that the opposite of love, hatred, should also be personal, for there is no one who loves who does not also hate.[22]

Do you want to embrace the terrible, wondrous beauty of God's holiness? Then run to Jesus. He will clothe you with the Spirit of God so that you will not be naked. Fly to the one whose name is Yahweh Saves and find a hiding place. Cry out to the Father and he will see his Son in you and will love you. This is the wonder of what God has done for us. When we realize how personal his wrath and hatred is for those who are sinful, then we can only be amazed at how personal his love and grace are for those of us whom he has called.

If you are called, if you have declared by the power of the Spirit that Jesus Christ is Lord, then be overwhelmed by the holy God who is alive and shown you great grace. For I am convinced that there is nothing so beautiful, so wonderful, so fearfully awesome as the Holy One. There is no better state to be in than holiness. I do not mean self-righteousness, but rather that place where you love the laws of God, knowing that what he has said is good, wholesome, and the right way. Surely this must bring contentment, for it is the opposite of burning with sin.

Recall the three men that have been mentioned in this chapter. When they realized God's presence and their own natures, they were terrified. But God showed great grace to them. God healed Job and blessed his latter years more than the former. Isaiah he cleansed of iniquities and sent him to speak the very words of God. Peter, though a denier and man of sin, was made into a fisher of men. Oh the wonderful grace of God which is greater that all our sin and shame! God be gracious to me, and transform me, a sinner! Let me not fear Your holiness, but glory in it and reflect it. Amen!

---

22. Lactantius, "Wrath of God," 69.

4

The Promise and Plan of Yahweh

"Such questions cannot be answered," said Gandalf. "You may be sure
that it was not for any merit that others do not possess: not for power or
wisdom, at any rate. But you have been chosen, and you must therefore
use such strength and heart and wits as you have."[1]

—THE LORD OF THE RINGS

THE QUOTATION FROM THE *Lord of the Rings* which begins this chapter
comes in one of the most telling part of the entire story. There is a foreshadowing of what must come: that Frodo must be the one to go on this quest to
destroy the Ring. Only a few paragraphs before, we get an inkling that the
creature Gollum will serve an important role in the completion of the great
task. It is a chapter filled with foreshadowing, of omens, and the weight of
this quest which has been thrust upon Frodo. As Gandalf says, there is no
reason Frodo should be the one to be the Ring Bearer. There is nothing in
Frodo that makes him the chosen one, and while he is a thoroughly good
hobbit, he has his faults. Gandalf has no better vision of the matter. He cannot say that Frodo is the best of all creatures in Middle Earth, even if he is
the best of hobbits. The only thing the wizard can say is that Frodo *has* been
chosen. But as a wizard he is, somehow, in connection with a deeper insight
into the wider world, and because of this he does not give over to agnostic

---

1. Tolkien, *Lord of the Rings*, 70

49

chance. He says that Frodo has been chosen, and though neither of them understands why, the little hobbit must do his best.

What goes unstated is exactly who had chosen Frodo. It was not Gandalf. It was not Sauron, or Gollum, or Bilbo. Even when elves, dwarves, and men are gathered at the House of Elrond and it is decided that the Ring must be destroyed, no one chooses Frodo. He volunteers, but only because he had already be been chosen. But by whom? And for what reason? Imagine if Elrond had told them that the maker of Middle Earth had chosen Frodo. What if he declared his name to be Tolkien? And what if he explained that the reason Frodo was chosen, the reason they had gathered, the reason for the quest and the reason for the Ring's existence at all was because this Tolkien wanted to tell a story and create a myth? Because in reality that is what the story is all about.

Viewing the story in this way does feel a little like looking the wrong way through a telescope. It seems to shift the weight of the story away from Frodo, Gandalf, and the rest of the fellowship, threatening to cheapen it all. But if done properly, we find this perspective is really looking the right way through the telescope, and instead of diminishing the story it expands it and gives all of it greater depth and meaning. After all, Tolkien crafted his masterpiece of English literature because *he* wanted to make it. But the difference between him and the creator of real earth is that Tolkien remains aloof. He is absolutely separate from his creation, though in every moment of the story his hand is moving it—from the flowing of the Anduin to the trickle of water in the land of shadow. The hope of the enemies of Mordor was that some nameless good might win.

There was no fellowship between Tolkien and his creation. As I said, he remained aloof, completely separate and, in a sense, holy. This holiness, though, is incomplete for it is never enjoyed by anyone, not even Tolkien. I suppose he never realized it, or cared to realize it. And it is exactly this which separates him from the creator of our world. For our Creator did not remain silent. He did not create and stay aloof. He loves his creation more than Tolkien loved his, for God *revealed* his holiness. He did not just keep it. Indeed, the revelation of his existence and his holiness was not accidental; and if it was not accidental, then it was purposeful. But the revelation of God's holiness at the same time manifests man's imperfection and sinfulness. Leaving things in this situation would do nothing but condemn. Fortunately, God shows us he has a different plan. It is a purpose and a plan for the world revealed in a promise, and it is through the unfolding of this plan, and the keeping of this promise, that God's Trinitarian nature is made known.

THE PURPOSE

There are two foundational facts that must be grasped concerning this plan of God. The first has to do with time. Some people, when speaking of what God is doing in the world, will see history as a series of failures, missed opportunities, and contingencies.[2] Not all of these are God's fault, but because of man's actions God has had to resort to backup plans. Israel, for instance, might have enjoyed all the benefits of God's promise, and they might have embraced their Messiah when he came humbly riding on a donkey. Jesus might not have died and would actually have ruled, even throwing off the burden of the Romans and setting up his own visible kingdom. But since the Jews rejected him, Christ died and God was forced to work through the church.

This, however, is not at all the perspective the Bible offers. Consider a passages from Paul's letter to the Ephesians.

> Blessed *be* the God and Father of our Lord Jesus Christ, who has blessed us with every spiritual blessing in the heavenly *places* in Christ, just as He chose us in Him before the foundation of the world, that we would be holy and blameless before Him. In love He predestined us to adoption as sons through Jesus Christ to himself, according to the kind intention of his will, to the praise of the glory of his grace, which He freely bestowed on us in the Beloved. In Him we have redemption through his blood, the forgiveness of our trespasses, according to the riches of His grace which He lavished on us. In all wisdom and insight He made known to us the mystery of His will, according to His kind intention which He purposed in Him with a view to an administration suitable to the fullness of the times, *that is,* the summing up of all things in Christ, things in the heavens and things on the earth. In Him also we have obtained an inheritance, having been predestined according to His purpose who works all things after the counsel of His will, to the end that we who were the first to hope in Christ would be to the praise of His glory. In Him, you also, after listening to the message of truth, the gospel of your salvation—having also believed, you were sealed in Him with the Holy Spirit of promise,

2. Kaiser, *Promise-Plan of God*, 30; Grudem, *Systematic Theology*, 860.

who is given as a pledge of our inheritance, with a view to the
redemption of *God's own* possession, to the praise of His glory. –
Ephesians 1:3–14 (NASB)

Notice what Paul says concerning God's timing of the choice. "He
chose us in Him before the foundation of the world." Then again he speaks
of the "eternal purpose" which was carried out in Christ. This eternality of
purpose and choice is not something that only exists in the future. It is not a
reference to time without end, but rather to a time before the world existed.
Long before we could do anything right or wrong, God had chosen to do
this thing in Christ. This means that what took place and what takes place
is not a contingency.

This leads directly in to the second point, and this is the specificity
of the plan. It is specific in its purpose, its mechanisms, and the persons
involved. Throughout the two passages under consideration is the witness
to Christ's central role in the work. While this may seem an almost insignificant thing, it really is not trivial. What is significant about it is that it
was a choice for blessing and adoption to come through Jesus Christ. It was
through his blood that redemption came to us. The wording here is not one
of surprise. Paul is not presenting these things as if some other outcome
might have occurred. No, it is clear that in Christ this eternal plan was to
be accomplished.

Aside from Christ there are other people specifically identified as being chosen. Paul says that God chose *us* in Christ before the foundation of
the world. This is not a selection of a faceless group. It is not an unpopulated
kingdom. The scripture is not saying that God chose Christians over Muslims or over Buddhist or even over atheist—as though religious preference
were akin to skin color. Paul says that God chose us in Christ, not that we
were in Christ therefore we were chosen. The choosing is of a more intimate
nature; as Paul says, "Christ loved *me* and gave Himself up for *me*."[3] The
apostle could never say this if Christ was just a sort of vacuum cleaner pick-
ing up whatever humans happen to be in the way. There is a purposeful
choosing and selecting which God does for his own purpose.

Naturally a question arises from this revelation. It is the question of
why. It is tempting to suppose this choice from eternity past was because
those chosen are particularly worthy of being chosen. Certainly Christ is
worthy of being chosen, and the explanation for this will be examined more
thoroughly in the chapter concerning God the Son. Let it suffice for now

3. Gal 2:20

to acknowledge that of all humans who have ever walked the earth none has been more worthy of special love and favor from the Father than Jesus Christ of Nazareth. But if we set him aside, accepting his worthiness, it must be asked whether any of those who are placed into Christ are worthy of being there. I say that we are tempted to answer in the affirmative, and that is because we hold ourselves in such high esteem and give ourselves too much credit. We think of ourselves as holy before God began sanctifying us. But this is a false notion, a deception of the heart, because Ephesians 1:4 makes it clear that it is only because God chose us in Christ that we can be blameless and holy before him. The value which differentiated us from other people came after the choosing and after our placement in Christ.

The plan and purpose of God is not something we deserve. There is another reason for it, and it is this: God has chosen to transform unholy humans into holy humans for the praise of his glorious grace. It is according to the riches of his grace that forgiveness has been granted by the holy God. Those who have been sealed with the Holy Spirit are sealed to the praise of his glory. Look over the passage from Ephesians again. Look for these statements and you will see that the driving purpose behind the blessing of humans in Christ is to glorify God and specifically to glorify his grace. Even the formation of the church and its administration are to display the wisdom of God, as Ephesians 3:10 says. The lives of the disciples individually and corporately, in their salvation and sanctification, are to make God look good.

This truth transforms the conversation about redemption and history by making man the object instead of the goal. What do I mean by this? I mean that it is not just for our sake that God is carrying out this purpose and plan. It is not as though he is obligated to enact redemption. Actually, it would make more sense for God simply to avenge his holiness on each of us right now, and rid his presence of those who seek to dethrone him. And to some he does this. Others he saves.

It might be said that the plan of redemption is for the sake of relationship. This is certainly true. The fact that God is acting in human history indicates he wants and has a relationship with us already, but our default relationship is one of wrath. The adoption as sons which Paul references is something special, and it is more than simply being God's creation. Being sons of God is something more intimate that our vileness should allow, yet it is an intimacy which is provided for in Christ. Why would God do this? The answer: to glorify his grace.

Is this right? Is this a good thing? Or is it self-aggrandizement and narcissism? Questions like this are why I think the focus of redemption and God's plan so often shifts to human beings. When it does, then we can accept the purpose; after all, human beings are worth saving—at least in our opinion. But this is simply our own narcissism, and we must avoid this mistake. We must not confuse God's purpose of glorifying his grace with the fact that we are beneficiaries of that grace. They are related, but they are not the same. We benefit from God choosing to glorify himself in this way, but benefiting is not the same as being the reason for the act. Perhaps it would be argued that if God was truly good then he would be altruistic and work to save us just because we exist. There would be no question of his glory, because that is not why he would save.

What this argument fails to appreciate is the eternal nature of the plan and God's place as Creator of the universe. In a word, this argument fails to appreciate monotheism. Too often when monotheism is considered it is pictured as the sweeping away of the many gods. Elizabeth Barrett Browning's poem "The Dead Pan" describes the death not only of the god Pan, but of all the other gods as well. This is the tragic hope of the entire poem, the thing fixated upon, and this is how we view monotheism. Our focus is too often on what is not there instead of who *is* there. There is God, who is the source of all existence. One could say he is the only really real thing that has ever existed because he depends on no one and nothing else to be alive. This, again, is the basis of his holiness. He is over and above all created things in his goodness, his truth, his power, his absolute and sole right to act. Press all these qualities and more to their maximum virtue and potency then ask why God has the right to act for his own glory. Press these things to perfection and then ask whether God must be altruistic. If He does not have the right to use his creation to glorify himself, then no child has the right to build and play with his LEGOs; no painter has the right to receive praise for a painting; and no carpenter has the right to live in a house which he has made.

What makes this difficult is that it makes us less that God. It makes us objects of his will. I don't mean inanimate objects, but animated and living tools for his purposes. At the heart of it, it means we are *creatures* and belong to a *creator*. We are things made, and have not existed from eternity to eternity. It means we have a purpose that is not our own and we are being used.

The only way to accept this is to embrace God's perspective. On one level we can never really do this because we are not and never will be God. We see but in a glass darkly. So we must rely upon what God reveals, and this is precisely what occurs in Ephesians. While not forsaking the benefit to humans, Paul again and again gives this perspective: what work God is doing he is doing to the praise of his grace.

THE PLAN AND THE PROMISE

This is the goal God is accomplishing. It is the motivating factor for what he is doing in human history—and he really is doing something. He is not merely giving us life every day like Mr. Rogers fed his fish every day. He is not just waiting for some sudden day of judgement. The goal he is accomplishing is not impersonal, but as we saw, has been extremely personal from eternity past. The means by which he is glorifying himself takes place in the movement of global history, of regional and nation history, of the history of families, and in the lives of individuals. He wants us to know about this, and the means by which he has revealed this purpose for the world is through a promise. As indicated in Ephesians 2:12, Gentiles were "separate from Christ, excluded from the commonwealth of Israel, and strangers to the covenants of promise, having no hope and without God in the world." What is interesting about this is that while Paul recognized the existence of multiple covenants, there is only a single promise. The same thing is present in Acts 26:6 where Paul, speaking before Agrippa, mentions a singular promise which Paul and the fathers of Israel had been given and clung to. As Willis J. Beecher points out, it is not promises, but a singular promise. "The whole essential messianic truth, as he [Paul] knows it he sums up in this one formula, 'the promise made of God unto our fathers.'"[4] This, according to Walter Kaiser, is the "central motif [around which] all the teaching of the New Testament (as well as the Old Testament) can be grouped."[5] All of the covenants, whether Adamic, Abrahamic, Mosaic, Davidic, or New Covenant, are pushing forward a singular promise. The beneficiaries of which have always been linked to it by faith in the progressive covenants. This is seen in Abraham when he believed God and it was accounted to him as righteousness. It is seen in the harlot Rahab who believed the promise so much that she hid the Israelite spies and betrayed her people.

4. Beecher, *Prophets and the Promise*, 180.

5. Kaiser, *Promise-Plan of God*, 20–21

So if these covenants are a part of a singular promise, what is the promise and what is God revealing about himself in giving it? Kaiser offers this explanation. "The promise-plan is God's word of declaration ... that God would continually *be* in His person and *do* in His deeds and works . . . His redemptive plan."[6] This promise-plan is the context in which the fullest revelation of God is being made. The promise, in other words, is himself: that *he* would do this thing for those who were once his enemies. He would fix the problem between us, at once satisfying holiness and yet drawing us near in friendship and sonship.

It makes sense that this should be God's plan, for if God's holiness and our unholiness are considered, then it seems almost a logical necessity that He should redeem humanity. To fail to do this would mean either the destruction of us or an eternal war between heaven and earth. Such a state would mean that God must always and forever hate his creation, and God's grace would never be praised.

The wonder of grace is brought into focus by the awesome terror of holiness. And both holiness and grace manifest in the specificity of how this redemption is to come about. With a single sentence God makes it clear how holy he is by saying in Ezekiel 18:2, "The soul that sins must die." In other words, life must be taken. The mechanism for life, in God's eyes, is revealed in Leviticus 17:11 which says that the life is in the blood. Therefore if a soul must die it means that its blood must be shed.

There is no more graphic depiction of seriousness and terror than bloodshed. To demand such a thing does not seem very gracious. It seems dreadfully demanding, even barbaric. But it is only barbaric when one loses sight of holiness. But when we remember this, it is impossible to see this handwriting of requirement as anything but an act of grace because the requirement has been revealed! We may think the system of sacrifice is barbaric, but it is really sin that is barbaric. God set up the system of sacrifice in order to show how holiness can be avenged. He created this system knowing full well that its ultimate satisfaction would be found in the blood of Messiah, the Son of God.

All of the signs and symbols of the law and covenants—from scripture itself to circumcision, the law, and the prophets—have the curious effect of focusing all of human history onto what we might consider purely religious matters. By this I mean that the movements of ancient empires such as Egypt, Assyria, Babylon, Persia, Greece, and Rome were ordered by God to

---

6. Kaiser, *Promise-Plan of God,* 19.

further his plan. Prophets like Isaiah understood this when foretelling that Cyrus was going to be raised up by Yahweh—a God Cyrus did not know or worship—as the instrument to bring his people back to the land. It was the conquest of Alexander that spread the Greek language throughout the Mediterranean world so that this became a common tongue and opened the word of God to people of other nations. It was the Roman Empire and its roadways which were the arteries down which the lifeblood of the gospel flowed. While the innumerable historical events of these different nations would seem enough to overshadow the few instances where God used them, we cannot let our vision become so obscured. It is just the sort of thing God would do: act in the least obvious way to rock the world. He always seems to do this, from choosing a man from Ur, to a group of slaves in Egypt, to investing all power, glory, and authority in a man from Nazareth, the boondocks of Judea. This same man, who was from nowhere Judea, was murdered outside the backward city of Jerusalem. But this plan did not stop at the hill outside of that city. Redemption has never been only about being saved from something. It is salvation *to* something. This is the underlying reality in all the covenants, but is especially evident in the Mosaic and New Covenants. In his grace God made a law expecting people to follow it. At first this might not seem like grace, but it clearly is. As God says in Deuteronomy 30:6, "The LORD your God will circumcise your heart and the heart of your descendants, to love the LORD with all your heart and with all your soul, that you may live." This is further clarified in Jeremiah 31:33 where it is written, "I will put My law in their minds, and write it on their hearts, and I will be their God, and they shall be My people." God is doing this thing, changing people and causing them to understand and do his will. This is exactly the principle Paul lays out in Ephesians 2:10 which says, "For we are His workmanship, created in Christ Jesus for good works, which God prepared beforehand that we should walk in them." This is placed in contrast with the lust of the flesh which Paul mentions only a few verses before—things which are against the law of God. So then we see that law itself is given by grace, for without it we would not know what it is to sin, and we would not know ourselves. We would also not know what is good and pleasing and the will of God.

The plan and purpose of God could be summarized in this way. Above all he is working so that his grace may be praised. He does this by clearly stating that the punishment for sin is death. He does it by enforcing this law, first by punishing Adam and Eve, but then by enforcing it upon humanity which continues to sin. God then was gracious in making a promise not to leave us in this state, but through a series of covenants began to add to and narrow the scope of the promise until we arrived at Christ. The sacrifice of Jesus of Nazareth satisfied the just punishment of those who are in him. Those who benefit from this work, from this promise, are always linked to it by faith, for without faith no one can please God. Finally, God continues to pour out grace upon grace through his Spirit which is working in us to produce good works. All of this is to the praise of his glorious grace.

IMPLICATIONS

This promise and plan of God is more than an agreement between God and the world, between God and men. It is an agreement God has made with himself. It was according to the council of his will, as Ephesians 1:11 says. This is what some theologians call the Covenant of Redemption.[7] Each member of the Trinity agreed to this, and took on particular roles for the glorification of God.[8] Of course, this is getting a little ahead of ourselves in the unraveling of the mystery, but not too far ahead. This Covenant of Redemption, this plan of God, is the context in which the Trinity is revealed, and the Trinity is what causes the whole redemptive plan to work and make sense.

The fact that God has revealed this plan and purpose should give us joy and hope. First, the hope hinges on God's intent to glorify his grace. He ties redemption to his receiving praise, and this should cause us to stop and consider something. Is God likely to fail at this goal of receiving praise? No! Each of us wants praise, particularly when we set out to accomplish something. So is it likely that God would say, "You'll praise me for I am going to do," and then not do it? No! Such a thing is absurd. God *will* glorify himself because he, more than anyone else, understands that he is worthy of praise and glory.

But God has not kept his plan a secret. He has interacted with us, giving us this promise. It is what has bridged the gap between the holy and the unholy. It is what bridges the gap between Creator and creation. It is a promise and work that is to give hope. It is the kind of hope that causes people to find joy even in the loss of a job. It gives strength to those suffering illness. It gives steadfastness in the turmoil of heartbreak. When

7. Hodge, *Outlines of Theology*, 271.

8. Grudem, *Systematic Theology*, 13

governments act wickedly, despising and persecuting the church, it is to this promise that the church should cling. A great cloud of witnesses have come before us, men and women long dead who went through trials and tribulations, persisting in them because they clung to faith. Faith in what? They had faith in the one living God and his promise, even though they had not yet received the thing promised.[9] Therefore we must do likewise, but with greater certitude, for the Lamb has been slain once for all time, and we have been given the seal of promise, the Spirit of God. We have been made part of the household of God, and know with certainty that the Father is putting all things under the feet of his Son.[10]

Such a promise provides us with a purpose. We are to glorify God, praising him for what Father, Son, and Spirit have done. We are to worship him, but not in words alone. Obedience to God is the destiny of those in the promise. More than whatever unique gifts each of us might have, and more than whatever great things he might do through each of us, we are called to simple obedience. It is obedience in the ordinary things in life. Fortunately, Paul lists several of them in the letter to the Ephesians. They are things like loving one another no matter if you're Jew or Gentile, man or woman, white, black, yellow, red, or purple. It is obedience in the family: husbands loving their wives as Christ loves the church, and wives submitting to their own husbands as the church to Christ. These simple things flow out of our understanding of the promise. That is because the promise of God is for us a worldview. The promise is what we have been given and provides the context for knowing God and knowing how to live. And it is in carrying out the promise that we come to know God and his unique nature as a Trinity.

9. Heb 11:39
10. Ps 110:1

5

The Revelator: God the Son

"For in place of the lamb, God appeared, and in place of the sheep a human being, and within the human being, the Christ, who contains all things."

—Melito of Sardis[1]

It began, as most things do, with a man claiming to be God. It is not really a unique thing in history. There have been many kings, rulers, and miscellaneous people who have claimed to be deity. The entire Pharaonic government of ancient Egypt was built upon this very idea. The deification of Caesar was a social and civic necessity. The claims by or for such men were the boastings of those who had taken or been given incredible power over people. It did not make them more than human, because the power they wielded was available to all men—but thank God only a few have grasped it! It is the kind of power every well known politician, every famous preacher, and every teenage social media stars wields: the power of personality and influence. The thing that has always made men into gods is the adoration, respect, and obedience of other people.

In the polytheistic world there were gods everywhere, and it made perfect sense that great men should be deified. Today, when the gods are dead or, worse, turned into Disney characters, no one becomes a god. Still, many strive for the same type of adoration, and not a few receive it. Yet

1. Melito of Sardis, "A Homily on Passover," 33.

if anyone actually claimed to be a god in all seriousness they would be laughed at or ignored by most people. If such a person persisted I suppose that they would be thought crazy, though in today's climate, it would not be surprising to me if we began to see an uptick in people identifying as deity. In our sinful state it is very likely that people will start talking about self-deification as a sort of positive-self exercise. Of course, this will carry about as much religious weight as vague spirituality and higher powers can carry—very little. That is because, for most of our culture, deity means very little. Ours is not a polytheistic society, but an atheistic one, where parts are rabidly against religious concepts, while others do not care one bit about it.

It is only in the monotheistic perspective that claiming to be God actually has any kind of meaning. Only monotheism places so much importance on the category of *deity* that if someone claims to be God it is something truly remarkable. I do not mean that anyone should actually believe a person claiming to be God—you likely shouldn't—but you really do need to pay attention. You have to make a decision, and as C.S. Lewis pointed out, there really are only three choices.[2] A person who claims to be the one, true God is either the most insane person on the planet, one of the most devilish liars who ever lived, or the Lord and Maker of the universe. And if anyone claims another human is God, then that person is either incredibly insane, remarkably gullible, are themselves devilish liars, or they are actually bearing witness to the truth.

When it comes to Jesus of Nazareth we are really dealing with this second scenario. None of us can claim to have walked with Jesus, to have touched him, or to have eaten with him as the disciples did. We are separated from this and recipients of a confession and a testimony. First John 1:1–3 indicates as much when it says, "That which was from the beginning, which we have heard, which we have seen with our eyes, which we have looked upon, and our hands have handled concerning the Word of life . . . that which we have seen and heard we declare to you." John's audience was composed of those who had not seen, touched, or heard. John was declaring the things that he had experienced for their benefit. So in trying to unravel the mystery of the Trinity it is necessary to acknowledge that the evidence is being presented by witnesses. It is the testimony of those who, as John says, saw heard and touched this man who made a rather incredible claim and in so doing revealed the Trinity.

2. Lewis, *Mere Christianity*, 50.

THE I AM STATEMENTS

As was said already, the revelation of the Trinity really began with a man claiming to be God. But how exactly would this be done in the context of monotheism? To avoid misunderstanding, to avoid the accusation of polytheism, such a person would have to make a claim to the divine name. If you recall from the chapter concerning Yahweh's monotheism, the phrase *I Am* became a name. This is clear in Exodus, but is evident in the book of Isaiah as well. There, God says that he will do certain things to make it clear that he is God alone, that *I Am* (Isaiah 41:4 and 43:10).[3] In the Greek Septuagint, the phrase is *ego eimi,* and the Septuagint would have been the text most familiar to the first century Christians. Of course, *ego eimi* could be used in contexts other than a claim to be God, as in the case of John 9:9. There, the blind man whom Jesus had healed was surprising everyone with his sight. Some were asking whether this was really the blind man. Others were saying it was just someone who looked like him. He who had been blind answered them by saying, *ego eimi.* This is like saying, "I am! I am!" Or, "I am he! I am he!" The NKJV says, "He said, 'I am *he,*'" whereas the NASB reads, "He kept saying, 'I am the one.'" In the Greek, the words are simply *ego eimi*: I am. The *he* or the *one* the translations use is implied in the sentence. The context of the blind man's statement clearly indicates he was only identifying as the blind man, and not making some claim to be the one God. So we must be careful in examining the context of the passage in order to understand what Jesus meant when he used the phrase.

We will look at the statements found in John 8. The first instance is in verse 24 which says, "Therefore I said to you that you will die in your sins; for if you do not believe that *ego eimi,* you will die in your sins." Now the Jews seem to have understood this in the way it is often translated, that is, that Jesus said if you do not believe that I am *he,* you will die in your sins. They responded by asking him, "Who are You?" This is only natural if they understood him to say I am *he.* They were thinking, *You are who*?

Jesus then makes another *ego eimi* statement by saying that when they have crucified the Son of Man they will realize that *ego eimi* and that Jesus does nothing of himself, but only what the Father has taught him. Maybe the Jews thought the *ego eimi* meant he was identifying as the Son of Man. After he said this, we are told that many believed in him. It is interesting,

3. For a discussion of the history of the term *"I Am"* especially in its use in the Greek Septuagint, see White, *Forgotten Trinity,* 98–100.

though, that instead of softening his rhetoric, instead of trying to reel them in, he pressured them. He told them were slaves. The Jews became angry or confused by this. Slaves? They had never been slaves, but were the children of Abraham. They were not Ishmaelites, children of slavery, but children of the freewoman Sarah. And Jesus continued to press them, and they got angrier and angrier, especially when He claimed to have seen Abraham. This was insane to the Jews. He was not even fifty, and had he seen Abraham? And it was just then that at last Jesus drove home the point He has been making: "Most assuredly, I say to you, before Abraham was, *ego eimi*."[4]

This time the Jews did not demand to know who Jesus was claiming to be. There was no need to ask. Suddenly they understood his other statements, how they would die unless they believed that he was *ego eimi*; how when he was raised up they would know he was *ego eimi*. Now that he claimed to be the I Am before Abraham they picked up stones. Why? It was not because he accused them of being sons of the devil. It was not because he claimed to speak the words of the Father. They were fine with that, especially if he was a prophet. The prophets often accused Israel of harlotry and unfaithfulness. The prophets certainly spoke the words of God; if they did otherwise they would have been false prophets. No, all of these things, while irritating, were not enough to cause them to fly into a zealous rage. And it was zeal for the law of God that stirred them up, because it says in Leviticus 24:16, "Whoever blasphemes the name of the LORD shall surely be put to death." To the Jews, Jesus being a man had made himself to be God by the statement *ego eimi*; he had just blasphemed the name of the LORD.

In any other culture of the ancient world Jesus might have been laughed off, or they might have shrugged and accepted his claim. Only to the Jews was it unacceptable. Their entire history as recorded in the Old Testament can be understood as a great pruning and purging by God to get rid of their tendency toward idolotry. From the Exodus through the Exile Yahweh was driving home one very important point: there was, is, and never will be any other God but Yahweh. Now this man from Nazareth comes along and claims not to be a god, but to be *the* God, to be Yahweh!

Of course, some people may suggest that the Jews had misunderstood Jesus throughout the conversation recorded in John 8. So how could they then be trusted to interpret Jesus' final claim correctly? This is a valid question, and if the rest of the scriptures did not bear witness to Jesus' claim,

4. John 8:58

63

then certainly there should be a great deal of hesitation on the part of Christians to say Jesus is Yahweh. But there is clarity offered in the scriptures, and briefly we will look at the witness of John and Paul to see what the New Testament declares about this Jesus.

THE TESTIMONIES OF JOHN AND PAUL

The texts which will be examined are John 1:1–5, 10–14 and Philippians 2:5–11. They are some of the loftiest passages in the entire New Testament, and they make important points concerning Christ's deity and his differentiation from the Father. They have several points in common, but their differences also tell us a great deal.

> In the beginning was the Word, and the Word was with God, and the Word was God. He was in the beginning with God. All things came into being through Him, and apart from Him nothing came into being that has come into being. In Him was life, and the life was the Light of men. The Light shines in the darkness, and the darkness did not comprehend it . . . He was in the world, and the world was made through Him, and the world did not know Him. He came to His own, and those who were His own did not receive Him. But as many as received Him, to them He gave the right to become children of God, *even* to those who believe in His name, who were born, not of blood nor of the will of the flesh nor of the will of man, but of God. And the Word became flesh, and dwelt among us, and we saw His glory, glory as of the only begotten from the Father, full of grace and truth.—John 1:1–5 and 10–14 (NASB)
>
> Have this attitude in yourselves which was also in Christ Jesus, who, although He existed in the form of God, did not regard equality with God a thing to be grasped, but emptied Himself, taking the form of a bond-servant, *and* being made in the likeness of men. Being found in appearance as a man, He humbled Himself by becoming obedient to the point of death, even death on a cross. For this reason also, God highly exalted Him, and bestowed on Him the name which is above every name, so that at the name of Jesus EVERY KNEE WILL BOW, of those who are in heaven and on earth and under the earth, and that every tongue will confess that Jesus Christ is Lord, to the glory of God the Father. — Philippians 2:5–11 (NASB)

One of the first things to notice is that both John and Paul shared an understanding that Jesus Christ was God before coming into the world. At the same time they both note a difference between Christ and God, meaning the Father. This is evident when John says that the Word was with God and when Paul says that Christ did not cling to being equal with God—both apostles meaning God the Father. The KJV and NKJV will say that he did not consider it *robbery* to be equal with God, and this might give a false impression because of the way the word *robbery* is used today. Today, if you commit a robbery, you are taking something that is not yours. But Jesus was not tempted to take something that was not his, for we are told that he was in the *form* of God. Theologian B.B. Warfield says, "'Form' is a term which expresses the sum of those characterizing qualities which makes a thing that it is. Thus the 'form' of a sword . . . is all that makes a given piece of metal specifically a sword rather than, say, a spade."[5] What Paul is saying, then, is that Christ possessed everything that makes God to be God. So if Christ already possessed it, then he could not steal or rob God of it. The idea, then, is that Christ did not clutch at being equal with God or try to hold onto it for his own sake though the form of God was rightfully his. This is why Paul can use Christ as an example of humility: in essence, Christ did not cling to his rights.

John makes the same point about Christ's deity when he says, "the Word was God." What makes this particular statement controversial to some people is the way it is written in the Greek. Jehovah's Witnesses will be quick to point out—and accurately I might add—that there is no article in front of *God* when it says the Word was God. Though the Greek article is not exactly the same as the English article, just to get an idea, this is what it might look like in English: "In the beginning was the Word and the Word was with *the* God and the Word was God." Jehovah's Witnesses would say that because the article is missing in front of God (it does not say that the Word was *the* God) that the text really should be understood to say, ". . . and the Word was *a* God." There is a good discussion about this in James White's book *The Forgotten Trinity*,[6] but it is sufficient for our purposes to use a little logic. First, John, being a Jew, was a monotheist in the absolute sense. There was, for John, only one God. So then it would seem we have an interesting paradox when it says that the Word was with God. Being with someone indicates you are not that someone, and if in the very next breath you say that you are that someone, well that doesn't make any sense, does it? So John cannot be saying that the Word was with God and that the Word

5. Warfield, "The Person of Christ," http://bbwarfield.com/works/person-of-christ/.
6. White, *Forgotten Trinity*, 47–64.

was that same person. What he must be saying (and the Greek bears this out) is the exact same thing that Paul is saying in Philippians. The Word possessed all the qualities of deity. If the phrase "the Word was with God" describes who the Word was with, then the statement "the Word was God" describes *what* the Word was.

Before moving to the next point where John and Paul agree, I first want to note a difference between them. It has to do with the name used for the Son in his pre-incarnate form. First, Paul says, "Have this attitude in you which was also in Christ Jesus. . ." He says that Christ Jesus existed in the form of God. Sometimes people think that Jesus Christ came into existence at the virgin conception or the virgin birth, but this cannot be the case if it was Jesus Christ who was in the form of God. Instead, it means that Jesus Christ existed before he took on flesh, before he was born as a man. All the *who* that was Jesus Christ existed before the *what* of his human flesh. This is not hard to understand if you consider it this way. Think of your mother or father or someone else you know. When you think of this person, do you think primarily of their body? If you do, then is it the same body from one memory to another? Probably not, nor should it be. The person took on different physical characteristics over time, and this does not matter. The person is more than flesh and blood, even in your memory. The physical is included, but the person is more than that physical nature. In the same way, the person who was and is Jesus Christ has never been limited to the physical, though as we shall see, this physical nature is an important part of the role he fulfills.

John gives a different name for the pre-incarnate Son. He uses the Greek term *logos*, which is usually translated *word* but can also mean *reason* or *thing*.[7] The concept of *logos* was not foreign to Greek philosophy, and it was given a Jewish spin in the hands of Philo of Alexandria. Philo described the *logos* as a being created by God who was then used as a sort of intermediary to create the physical universe.[8] This sounds strange, but Philo was not pulling things out of the blue. The idea of *logos* is present in the scriptures. After all, "God said let there be . . ." and whatever he commanded came into being. Psalm 33:6 says that by the power of his word the heavens and earth were made. And according to Psalm 107:20 it is by the power of God's word that the people are healed. In these verses it is clear that the

7. White, *Forgotten Trinity*, 49. White does not mention *idea* in his possible translation, but since words carry ideas, it seems appropriate to draw the connection.

8. Gonzalez, *History of Christian Thought Volume I*, 45.

word is power and action, but John is revealing something startling. The Word is not merely a sound carried through the air or letters on a page. According to John, this Word is a person, and this person is God. This Logos is the one who created the world, as John 1 tells us, "without him nothing was made that was made." Again in Colossians 1:16–17, "all things were made through him and for him and in him all things hold together."

As Christians we like to talk about creation being merely by the power of God's spoken word, but there is no *merely* about it. This is no idle babble or curious sound. It cannot even be compared to the most eloquent piece of literature, for our words are imperfect and vanish like the mist. But if there was a word that was perfect and powerful this would constitute something completely different. Think of it this way. If I try to describe myself in words I will do so imperfectly. If I were to spend several paragraphs describing my history, my physical characteristics, and even try to tell you what I think, you will have a woefully inadequate picture of who I am. This is because my words are imperfect. All of human communication, whether written or spoken, is imperfect. But what if the words were perfect? What if they could express me clearly and completely? Truly, if the words were perfect, then there would need to be only one word which would express me. This word, if it was perfect, would not and could not merely be vibrations in the air or ink on a page. As the perfect expression of who I am, it would be me. There would be no gaps open, no interpretation required. You would know me by the word of my communication as perfectly as if it was me standing before you.

Of course, this is really hard to understand, but I think it is important. The Son is the *Logos*, the perfect word or idea of God.[9] This is why it can be said in John 1:18, "No one has seen God at any time; the only begotten God who is in the bosom of the Father, he has explained Him."[10] The Son has explained the Father because he is the *Logos*, the perfect communication of God. To be perfect in the truest sense means complete and full, not missing anything. This includes personhood and deity. Everything that the Father possesses the Son also possesses perfectly. There is such harmony,

9. Jonathan Edwards in his "Discourse on the Trinity" provides an insightful discussion of what it means for the Son to be the idea of God, that is, God's perfect self-contemplation. One must be careful in reading Edwards not to make the mistake of thinking Jesus is either (1) a created person, or (2) *only* the idea of God as thought this made Him less real and less God than the Father.

10. There is a textual variant here, for texts such as the NKJV will read, "The only begotten Son" as opposed to the NASB which says, "The only begotten God."

such perfect expression that Jesus can say in John 12:45, "He who sees Me sees the One who sent Me," and again in John 14:8, "He who has seen Me has seen the Father." Jesus is not saying he *is* the Father, but he is the perfect expression of the Father. He is the radiance of the Father's glory and the exact representation of his nature.

This last statement concerning Christ is found in Hebrews 1:3, and the word used for *representation* in the NASB is given as *image* in the NKJV and *stamp* in the RSV. The RSV actually presents a more literal rendering, because in Greek the term was employed in the making of an image or copy of the original, often having to do with a stamp for coins or a seal impressed in wax. Some people, wanting to deny Christ's diving nature or shared nature with the Father, will argue that a copy never shares the age of the original. If you make a photo copy of a document, then the copy will never be as old as the original document. The physical characteristics of the original are transferred, but not the age or life-span of the original. In the same way, they argue, if Jesus is the image or copy of God, he cannot be eternal because he must have come into existence at a point in time. And if he is not truly eternal, then he is not truly God. What this argument fails to appreciate is that even with paper copies, the temporal nature *is* transferred from original to the copy. The copy had a beginning just like the original, and it will have an end just like the original. Whether one exists for twenty years and the other for two hundred is of no difference. The fact remains that they have a temporal existence: a beginning and end. In the same way a "copy" of God that is a true copy, containing all the fullness of deity, would share God's temporal nature; that is, the copy of God would be eternal, without beginning or end. In the same way the copy of an object bound by time remains bound by time (having beginning and end), so too the copy of the eternal would also be eternal (without beginning or end).

The key to understanding this difficult concept lies in perfection: the perfection of God and the perfection of the Logos. For God to do a thing perfectly is to do it completely; therefore, if he was to communicate himself perfectly and fully, then that communication must be as whole and complete as he is. In the same way, if the Logos is perfect in the fullness of his communication (to such an extent that to see him is to the see the Father), then the Logos must be God. This means that God was not silent until suddenly speaking the Word into existence. The Logos existed and was in fellowship with the Father before the world was, as Christ's prayer in John 17 indicates. God has never been silent for his Word always has existed.

When Christ is understood as the Logos, the communication of God, then it should make sense why he was the one who was incarnate. Just as our own words bridge the gap between author and audience, so too the Word of God bridges the gap between God and man. This meant leaving the divine realm and entering the world of men. As John says, "The Word took on flesh and dwelt among us." Paul says, "He [Christ] made Himself of no reputation, taking the form of a bondservant and coming in the likeness of men." Paul uses the same idea of *form* he used to describe Christ's deity. Christ took on all the qualities of a servant as a human. For John, the Word took on flesh, the nature of a human being. Thus Christ was fully God and fully man.

Now this idea of taking on flesh is rather difficult to understand. After all, there is an infinite difference between the infinite and the finite. Men can never level up to be God—though, I think, the Mormon Church does actually teach that it can be done. So there is a temptation to say that Jesus only looked like a man, that He was just wearing a human suit like the alien wearing an Edgar suit in the movie *Men in Black*. But this kind of piety is in error because it starts from the wrong spot by recognizing that finite man can never become the infinite God. The right starting point, the right question to ask is whether the infinite, all powerful God can take on the finite nature of man. Can God do this thing? The Muslim answer is no. Their god, Allah, cannot do this. The biblical witness is that yes, Yahweh can do this, and has done it in the man Jesus of Nazareth. The trouble most people have with this lies in an assumption, and that assumption is based on a fallacy. They think that to be a sinner is to be human and therefore to be human is to be a sinner. This is not the case. The perfect human nature does not possess sin, or rather, is not possessed by sin. So Christ, in being perfect, did not become sin in the sense of becoming a sinner in heart, soul, mind, and strength. He could not hate God, or that would go against his existence as the Logos, as God. But, some would ask, if he really was perfect, how could He possibly have dwelt in a human body? Did he not get hungry? Did he not need a diaper change? Did he not experience growing pains? Did he not need sleep or even to relieve himself? How could he, being perfect, have dwelt in such an imperfect house? The answer is that the Old Testament reveals a God willing to tabernacle in a tent made of skins carried around in the desert. What difference is it that this human tabernacle ate, excreted, needed sleep, could be wounded, or even killed? I think we have a false sense of what perfection looks like. We think our bodily functions are innately sinful, but if Jesus ate and drank, produced waste and needed sleep, then we must assume that to be the perfect human is still to do these things.

Nevertheless, to take on the human form when one had known only the divine is an incredibly humbling act on God's part, and this is Paul's point in Philippians. In all the glory that is God, in all the righteous zeal for his holiness, he also possesses infinite humility. It is not that he has humility in a certain percentage. This would never work, because the gap between the infinite and the finite is too great. To transcend the boundary between heaven's glory and the dark world of men required infinite humility. This is the role, this is the quality God the Son chose to display in becoming a man. It is awesome. He humbled himself to become the door, as He says in John 10:9, and just as a door has two sides and yet is one door, so too Jesus has two natures and is yet one person.

To do this thing, Jesus had, in a very real sense, to make himself nothing. The NASB translation of Philippians says that Christ "emptied" himself, and this might be a little misleading because Christ did not cease being God. Perhaps this emptying consisted of a kind of limiting, such as is described in Matthew 24:36 when no one, not even the Son, knew the day or the hour of that ultimate and final Day. Augustine believed that there were certain divine actions or knowledge that Christ chose not to access; much like Paul chose to know nothing among the Corinthians except Christ crucified.[11] While I am not sure that Augustine is correct, what is certainly true is that Christ did not cease being God. We do know that he veiled his glory so that, in accordance with Isaiah 53:2, he should have no form or comeliness. But if he lost even the smallest percent of the infinite, perfect divine nature, then He could no longer be God. So the emptying, I think, has more to do with clutching at divine glory than actually setting aside divinity. Jesus was not "self-regarding: he had regard for others."[12] In humbling himself, in taking on flesh, Jesus acted to serve God and so did not cling to and use those options which were available to him. This is the temptation he faced in the wilderness when the devil told him to change the stones to bread. The devil was not saying, "I bet you can't do this." Instead, he was saying, "I know you can do this, so do it!" Jesus' answer was one of incredible discipline and humility, for he persisted in not grasping hold of the divine prerogative even when he was hungry. He did this because he loved the Father. And this obedience, this humility would lead to death on the cross.

11. Augustine, *On the Trinity* 1.12.23
12. Warfield, "The Person of Christ," 4.

So, as you can see, these two small passages from Paul and John are filled with all sorts of things. They differ in some points on what they focus on and reveal, but they provide a unified picture of Christ. While the two apostles differ in focus, one can see a common foundation. That foundation is that Jesus Christ is God, and that He took on the human nature. By doing this he was obedient to the Father and served as the central player in the drama of redemption.

THE SON'S ROLE IN THE PLAN OF GOD

It is impossible to separate the revelation of the Son from his work in redemption. His role in the plan of God glorifying himself and his grace began not in the tomb, or on the cross, or even in the manger. It began with his agreement with the Father to be the Lamb of God. This is something that he did willingly. Paul's passage in Philippians is itself proof that Christ willingly emptied himself and took on the form of a servant. If Paul was to successfully use Christ as a model of humility, then Christ must have acted humbly and not by humiliation. He chose to do it; it was not forced upon him. This agreement was, as I Peter 1:20 points out, before the world was created. Christ was foreordained before the foundation of the world as the lamb that would be slain. The eternal nature of this choice shows us that the idea was not sprung on him suddenly. As God in the fullest sense, no one could have forced him to do it or surprised him by it.

These things prove the eternal choice of the Son to take a particular role. His willingness to go through with it is first manifest in the creation of the world. As John 1 tells us, the Word is the Creator of everything made that has been made. Colossians goes a step farther and says that everything holds together in Christ. Had the Son not been willing to engage in the plan of God, he would never have participated in this beginning act. But he did participate, and intimately so as the Logos.

As has already been mentioned, throughout the scriptures, God's word is associated with power and action, and it seems probable that the Son is himself in mind when in Genesis chapter one God speaks the universe into being. This brings a new understanding to God's creative power by word if in this case *word* is a person and not vibrations in the air. Truly it is as Melito of Sardis said, "He who hung the earth is hanging. He who fixed the heavens in place has been fixed in place. He who laid the foundations of the universe has been laid on a tree." Surely the Son would have known what he was creating and for what purpose, and so this puts to rest all criticisms of the cross which say it was the ultimate act of child abuse. Only if the Son was an unconscious or ignorant person could this be the case, but the picture painted in scripture is not of an ignorant Creator.

Aside from creation, the Son as the Logos has served in history to reveal God. The Gospel of John tells us that no one has seen God at any time. This is a strange statement considering Abraham, Moses, Elijah, and Isaiah all saw God is some way. John is either ignorant of these instances—which is unlikely—or he is telling us something important. And indeed, he demonstrates what this thing is. It is a differentiation between God the Father and God the Son. No one has seen God *the Father* at any time. The Son of God declares the Father and it is he who the men of old saw. When, in Isaiah 6, the prophet is recorded to have seen Yahweh, who does John claim he saw? It was Jesus.[13] It should come as no surprise that this is the case when Christ's nature as Logos is taken into account. If anyone was going to see the glory of God, the expression of God even in the Old Testament, they must have seen the Son, the Logos.

The Son not only serves to communicate in this way, but also in a more immediate sense by taking on flesh and entering the world of men. The Logos no longer communicates at a hierarchical difference with a clear distinction between God and man, but bridged the gap by becoming a man. He veiled his glory so that the eyes of men might behold him, and their ears be saved from his thunderous voice. His flaming raiment and brazen skin now became touchable and able to be handled. And handled he was, in the most barbarous fashion: handled not out of love or affection or worship, but with insults and murderous intention.

This murderous intention was not outside of God's purpose, for death was required. This was the plan all along, and communicated in history via the law and the sacrificial system. God's offended holiness demanded the death of the sinner's soul. This was the holy paradox set up by God: he will not yield his holiness and yet he wants a people in whose midst he will dwell. So, in order to glorify his grace, God sent his only Son who came willingly to serve as that satisfying sacrifice. It had to be him, for no mere man would do. The breach was too great between God and man: the finite could not bridge the infinite. The imperfect could not approach the perfect.

It is fascinating that in the Old Testament there is never given a once-for-all sacrifice. Yes, there existed a system whereby again and again the

13. John 12:41

72

people's sin could be covered for a time, but there was never any finality about it. As the author of Hebrews says, "[I]t is not possible that the blood of bulls and goats should take away sins."[14] What the law did not command was human sacrifice, and a moment's consideration reveals why. No ordinary man would have sufficed. No matter how honorable, how pure, how much a man after God's heart he might be, his sacrifice would be ineffectual, for his death would be merely deserved. Choose any Old Testament saint: Enoch, Noah, Moses, David, Elijah, or any of the prophets and you will find men who were imperfect. Choose the most noteworthy person either mentioned or unmentioned in the listed of faithful people of Hebrews 11 and you will have someone full of faith, but not someone who was sinless. They will have lived their lives and will have broken the law of God. Even go to the extreme. Choose a child who has not lived long enough to commit any kind of sin. Even then the sacrifice would be imperfect because no child loves Yahweh with all of his heart, soul, mind, and strength. No child is so holy; no child is so perfect.

Only Christ and his blood would serve to cover over the sins of men and women once and for all. This is because the life he lived, and the life contained and symbolized by his blood, was perfect. It is not just that he was nice or "did the right thing," as if this was something anyone could do. At a very fundamental level he was unlike anyone else who ever lived, for he never sinned. He never sought to dethrone God; he only ever and always loved God.

The magnitude of what this means is found in what Paul says in Philippians 2:8, where we are told that being found in appearance as a man Christ became obedient to the point of death—even the horrid, shameful death of the cross. This obedience was necessary on the part of the Son because he had taken the human nature to himself. The human nature is, fundamentally, less than God. So in its perfect expression the human must be submissive to God. It was necessary for the Son to be perfect on the human level, to fix that relationship between God and man, so that he might become the perfect sacrifice. It was absolutely necessary for him to say in all things, "Father, thy will be done." For this reason we see throughout the Gospels, and especially in John, that Jesus only did the will of him who sent him. To do anything else, even in the slightest regard, would have disqualified him. But it was not a burden, because as the eternal Logos he already

14. Heb 10:4

had always done the will of him who sent him. Therefore being both sinless and God-loving, Jesus had righteousness to spare.

Think about what kind of love the Father must have for this obedient Son! And just consider the love the Son has for the Father! For at the heart of the creation, incarnation, and passion is not just love for man, but ultimately, love for God. It is a love and glory which the Son had always known. He was and is the Beloved Son, as the Father himself testified. And yet, in becoming the sacrifice for sins, he bore the wrath of God. In becoming the sacrifice he became sin. As it is written, "He became sin for us who knew no sin." So in that terrible, eternal moment when the Son bore the sins of many, he became like one hated.

Can we imagine such a terrible and dramatic change? To go from Beloved to Hated is the greatest change that can take place! And if he became sin, then in the eyes of God, in the presence of his holiness, only hatred was rightfully due to that object of sin. But the Son willingly did this. For the sake of love He bore divine hatred. With every action he declared, "Father, I love you!" And in the heat of wrath he said to his people, "I love you."

Christ loved us so much that He allowed us to die. It was a death of shame, a death of agony, a death to sin. Here, at this point, we are in him. The sacrificial system of animals could never do what Christ has done. We were never incorporated into the lamb's death. Its blood only temporarily covered the sin for those it was sacrificed for, and there could be no part in it. For if anyone should be incorporated into the death of the lamb he would find himself made even less that he is now: instead of being a sinful man, God would see an animal. So no man could take part and be incorporated into the death of an animal, for an animal has no power to save. In the same way a mere man has no power to save, for even if he was sinless in himself there is no power to be raised up to God in this. There would remain a gulf of separation between the perfect man and the infinite God. And this is why the Trinity is important. Christ, being God and man, has the ability not only to bear wrath, but to raise us up with him beyond the gulf. He united men not only with a perfect man, but with the God-man, and if we are united with the God-man, then now we are united with God.

The Son is the Savior, for in uniting us to himself he rescues us from the wrath that is to come, for if we are in him, then the wrath that was due to us has been spent upon him. Because he is both God and Man there is no doubt in his ability to save. He is the Beloved. Is there any doubt that the Father will hear his intercession? And indeed, the Son is risen from the dead and makes intercession for those who are his, as it says in Hebrews 7:25, "Therefore He is able to save to the uttermost those who come to God through Him, since He always lives to make intercession for them."

He lives! Having defeated death the Son has defeated every possible enemy. There is nothing more that can be done to him. Nothing can conquer him; in all the world, in all the universe, there is nothing more potent than death. Even beyond the world, beyond the last star, to the highest heaven there is only one power ever able to destroy: the wrath of God, and that was spent upon him! Not in a failed attempt, but in a successful attempt the wrath was poured out completely and the Son drank the cup. Oh bitter draught never tasted by many who deserved it! It was emptied by the Son! Death, where is your victory? It is swallowed up in the victory of the Son of God!

Sometimes Christians have a tendency to over spiritualize things, and by this I mean we banish them from the realm of reality to that of pious imagination. But the victory of the Son of God over death is not just spiritual. Salvation is not just spiritual. It is weighty, and as fleshy as the body that still bears the scars of the cross. It is a powerful and living reality. As it is written in John 6:39–40, "This is the will of the father who sent Me, that of all things He has given Me I should lose nothing, but should raised it up at the last day. And this is the will of Him who sent Me, that everyone who sees the Son and believes on Him may have everlasting life, and I will raise Him up at the last day." Again, in John 10:28 it is written, "I give them eternal life, and they shall never perish; neither shall anyone snatch them out of My hand." These are not just nice, spiritual things to say. This is the reality of what is and what *will* be.

Settle this firmly in your heart and mind. This same one who created the heavens and the earth, the one who was perfect in obedience, offered himself freely and justly, this one who died once for all, this one who took his life back up defeating death forever, this one to whom all things even death will bow down to is the same one in whose hands you have been placed, if you are truly his. And who can defeat him? Who can pry open his hand? He has so completely fulfilled his work that his work is no longer outside of himself, but has been made a part of his body. So do you want assurance of salvation? Do not place it in a prayer or a feeling of being close to God, for prayers end and feelings fade. Instead, place your hope in the one whose job it is to hold on forever to those who have been given to him. Place your hope in God the only Son because that is the role he has taken!

All hopes and all fears find their focus in the Son. He has been given a name which is above every name and at the name of Jesus every knee will bow and every tongue confess that Jesus Christ is Lord. This is nothing less than the fulfillment of Isaiah 45:22–23 which says, "Look to Me, and be saved, all you ends of the earth! For I am God, and there is no other. I have sworn by Myself; the word has gone out of My mouth in righteousness, and it shall not return, that to Me every knee shall bow, every tongue shall take an oath." And again, this is not merely a messianic statement. It is Yahweh speaking. And this same monotheistic statement is applied to Jesus so that there is not a king on earth, not a president or congress, not a governor or mayor or any other human authority who is outside of his authority. This is the role the Son has taken. As it is written in Psalm 110:1, "The LORD said to my Lord, 'Sit at My right hand till I make Your enemies Your footstool.'" And the nations are warned in Psalm 2:12, "Kiss the Son, lest He be angry, and you perish in the way, when his wrath is kindled but a little. Blessed are those who put their trust in Him."

As Ruler of all rulers the Son is also the judge of the living and the dead.[15] This is a function tied to his incarnation, for all men will look into the face of their judge. As it is written in Revelation 1:7, "Behold, he is coming with the clouds, and every eye will see Him, even they who pierced Him. And all the tribes of the earth will mourn because of Him." That the Son does this reveals the righteous judgement of God, for in this way the judge is not invisible in heaven, but visible in flesh on the earth. There is justice in this, for men will not be accused and condemned by a faceless force. To those of us who are his, to at last see him face-to-face will be a wonder and a joyous occasion. To see him at last unveiled in all the glory of God will be a sight too wonderful to describe! At the same time it will be a terrible sight for the wicked, for they shall see him the same way. There will be no excuse, no doubting, and they will no longer be able to hide. They too shall see him who was pierced, and they will mourn.[16]

This is who Jesus of Nazareth claimed to be, and who his disciples declared him to be. It is easy to be caught up in it without realizing what is happening. Not only is it revealed who Jesus really is, but who God is, and what he is like. In all the discussion about creation and redemption and the culmination of all things, the spotlight is on Jesus. He is very much the front-man of God. But like all good front-men, he draws attention to

15. Acts 10:42.

16. Augustine, *On the Trinity*, 1.3.30

himself and to the rest of the band. In the same way, in all that Jesus is, has done and will do, he reveals the Father. He has also revealed the Spirit, and has sent the Spirit from the Father. So in the revelation of the Son the brightest of lights has dawned upon the world, and it shone first in a filthy manger.

Now looking back over this chapter I cannot help but feel my attempt to communicate the wonder of the Son has been inadequate. There is so much wrapped up in who he is—not just regarding our salvation, but also concerning the world and wisdom, of communication and life, and God's very nature. It is overwhelming, if only I can keep it in mind. The old song that says, "Turn your eyes upon Jesus, look full in his wonderful face, and the things of earth will grow strangely dim in the light of his glory and grace," is so very true. It is true if we use the eyes of our mind to consider what has been revealed of the Son by the witnesses who saw him, walked with him, learned from him, and were sent by him. When Paul writes, "Finally, brethren, whatever things are true, whoever things are noble, whatever things are just, whatever things are pure, whatever things are lovely, whatever things are of good report, if there is any virtue and if there is anything praise worthy—mediate on these things,"[17] I cannot help but think that in saying this, he had the Son of God on his mind. For who else is true? Who else is noble? Who else is just, pure, lovely, and of good report? Who else is full of virtue and absolutely praiseworthy? Is it not the Beloved Son of God? And truly, when our minds feast upon this, everything does seem somehow to grow dim, and when we have realized their dimness it will not seem strange to us. For the Son shines brighter and the Son's light is warmer even than the sun in the sky. He is the glory of God, and all else pales in comparison.

17. Phil 4:8

6

The Originator: God the Father

"Our Father in heaven,
Hallowed be Your name.
Your kingdom come.
Your will be done
On earth as it is in heaven"

— MATTHEW 6:9b-10

VERY FEW PEOPLE HAVE ever argued that the Father is not God. There does not ever seem to have been the same kind of theological wrangling about the Father as there has been about the Son, and this is because to some extent God has always been viewed as a sort of father. A few times God is referred to as father in the Old Testament and those instances will be examined momentarily. However, what needs to be understood is that there is a difference between God as father and God the Father, for Christ does not merely reveal God as father—which he did not really need to reveal—but that there is a person identified by the name *Father* within the Trinity. His role is different from Son's in that he is the originator and head of God.

THE FATHER DIFFERENT THAN THE SON

The idea of God as father is not something unique to the New Testament. In a sense, the creative act itself is a fathering act. All human beings, by

78

nature of creation, are children of God because he created us. However, it is clear that when the scriptures speak of anyone being a child of God it is almost always in a special, chosen sense, and not in a general one. Isaiah 64:8 provides just such an example when it says, "But now, O LORD, You are our Father, we are the clay, and You our potter; and all of us are the work of your hand." In Deuteronomy 14:1–2 Israel is said to be, ". . . sons of the LORD your God." So fatherhood was more than physical creation, and carried with it a special kind of relationship with God.

Another example of this special fatherhood is found in Isaiah 63:16 where the prophet says, "Doubtless You are our Father, though Abraham was ignorant of us and Israel does not acknowledge us. You, O LORD, are our Father, our redeemer from everlasting is Your name." It is very interesting that immediately following this the prophet, speaking for the people, asks why God has hardened their hearts and removed his presence from them. They became like those who had never known God and were his enemies. There is a striking parallel—or perhaps a fulfillment—in John 8:12–14 which was examined in the previous chapter. Our interest then was upon Jesus' claim to be God, but now we will focus on what revelation is made about the Father.

The issue of descent and sonship comes after Jesus said that if the Jews abide in his words then he would make them free. They bristled at this insinuation, stating that they were Abraham's descendants and had never been in bondage to anyone. It is possible that they were foolish enough to have forgotten about Egypt, Assyrian, Babylon, and Rome, but I doubt it. Instead, they really do seem to have understood Jesus to have been directing them toward inner freedom; thus they claimed Abraham as their father. Some of them probably had an ancient song going through their heads: "Father Abraham had many sons, and many sons had father Abraham. . ." No doubt they had begun the *left foot, right foot, turn around sit down* part, but others were brooding about what Jesus was saying. Of course Abraham was their father! He was their father by blood and by covenant. What did this upstart mean? "I know that you are Abraham's descendants, but you seek to kill Me, because My word has no place in you," continued Jesus. Yes, they were genealogically descended from Abraham, but he was not really their father. They were not like him, for, as he said, "I speak what I have seen with My Father, and you do what you have seen with your father."[1] Of course the Jews snapped back with, "Abraham is our father!"

1. John 8:38.

Again Jesus pressed them, replying that if they were Abraham's children then they would do what Abraham did. They would have rejoiced to hear the truth, but now they sought to kill him, something Abraham never did. Then he says again, "You do the deeds of your father."

Furious, the Jews take a swipe at Jesus, "We were not born of fornication," as if to say Jesus was born of fornication. Virgin birth indeed! Who knows the name of Jesus' father, but they were quite willing to say of themselves, "We have one Father—God."[2] Having cast aside the issue of blood and genealogy, they claimed to have a special relationship with God. They identified with the Torah and the covenant, and in essence identified with what Isaiah had said. That they moved past Abraham (Abraham did not know us) to claim God as Father, was nothing to Jesus. He just pushed them farther along in the Isaiah passage. They were not really of God, but where like those who never followed the Torah and were never called by God's name. Jesus, on the other hand, did the will of God whom he called "My Father."[3]

Throughout John 8 Jesus identifies one whom he calls both God and Father. At first this garnered little reaction from the Jews because they did not know who he was talking about (as John points out in verse 27). Then, when they claimed God as their father, Jesus turned that aside and said, "No, God is *My* Father." It culminates with Jesus claiming to be *I Am*, as was covered in the last chapter. The important point is just there, though, for when Jesus claims to be Yahweh he reveals something not only about himself, but also about this Father and God he had been referring to. It is not just that God could be considered a father, because that had been known in the Old Testament. It is, as B.B. Warfield said, "The mystery of the Trinity is not revealed in the Old Testament."[4] It is only in the revelation of the Son that at the same time there is a revelation of the Father, for the Jews understood that the God to which Christ appealed as Father was the one God of the covenant: Yahweh. So at the very moment when Jesus says, "Before Abraham was, I Am" he forces us to consider this strange idea about God. It is not that he is the Father, but that the Father is someone and Jesus is someone, and both make a claim to be the one God.

Just glance back over John 8. In verse 18 Jesus says the Father bears witness of him. What is curious is that he is making a point about the law

2. John 8:41

3. John 8:29, 49, 54

4. Warfield, "Trinity," bbwarfield.com/works/trinity.

requiring two witnesses. Jesus claims to be one witness and the Father another witness. The Jews obviously understood him to be referring to another person because in the next verse they ask, "Where is your Father?" Also in verse 18 Jesus says that the Father not only bears witness of Jesus, but was the one who sent him. Surely, if Jesus and the Father were the same person, then Jesus would have said nothing about being sent, but would have talked about coming of his own accord. But if there is one thing that he is adamant about in this chapter it is that he does not do his own will, but the will of the one who sent him. And because he always does what pleases the Father, the Father has not left him alone.[5] This makes absolutely no sense unless the Father was another person.

This is one of the major clues in our theological mystery about God, and it is found throughout the New Testament. The Father and the Son are distinct, and the biblical authors mention it almost in passing, which is itself an important clue. The apostles and other writers simply state something already incorporated into their thinking. As Warfield says, "[The New Testament] is not a record of the development of the doctrine [of the Trinity] or of its assimilation. It everywhere presupposes the doctrine as the fixed possession of the Christian community."[6] This is nowhere more clearly illustrated than in Paul's letters. In Galatians 1:1 he claims to be an apostle through Jesus Christ and God the Father. This is then followed by something he includes in almost every letter. He says, "Grace to you and peace from God the Father and our Lord Jesus Christ." Sometimes he changes the wording to say God *our* Father and the Lord Jesus Christ.[7] This is often followed by a blessing or thanksgiving passage such as is found in Ephesians 1:3 which says, "Blessed be the God and Father of our Lord Jesus Christ . . ." What this illustrates is that Paul understood the Father and Jesus to be distinct.

Now, there are some who contend that when Paul says something like, "the God and Father of our Lord Jesus Christ," he thus indicates that Jesus is not divine. This is, of course, nonsense, because as has already been discussed, in Philippians 2 Paul's very argument is that Jesus existed in the form of God and therefore was God. So it must be understood that in Paul's writings there is a distinction between the Father and Jesus, but both are God.

5. John 8:29
6. Warfield, "Trinity," bbwarfield.com/works/trinity.
7. Eph. 1:2; Phil. 1:2; Col. 1:2

Other writers also noted this distinction. There is the opening of James where he claims to be the bondservant of God and of the Lord Jesus Christ. Then there is Peter who writes, "Blessed be the God and Father of our Lord Jesus Christ . . ."[8] Jude writes, "To those who are called, sanctified by God the Father, and preserved in Jesus Christ."[9] Once again the evidence shows us that the Father and Son are not the same person, but they are both God.

THE ROLE OF THE FATHER

So what is to be understood about the Father? One of the first things to note is that he is the Father of our Lord Jesus Christ. This is relational. In the Gospels, Jesus constantly refers to the Father as *his* Father. And the Son does whatever he sees the Father do. To say he learns from the Father gives the wrong impression, for since he is God Jesus already knows everything. Instead, the Father seems to be the source of the Son, for Jesus is the *only begotten* of the Father. It is not that the Son is created by the Father so that at some point in creation-time the Father became the Father and the Son became the Son. It is an eternal state, an eternal relationship, though it is expressed in the redemptive incarnation. It is nearly impossible to describe in physical or physiological terms what exactly is being expressed. The closest thing we can come to is to refer back to the discussion of Christ's nature as the Logos. The Son is the communication of God in that he communicates the Father. In this way the Father is the Originator of the communication, though he is not the Communication himself. This is the relationship between the Father and Son: the one the eternal communication and the other the eternal communicator.

One of the implications of this relationship is that the Father has the role of authority not only among men, but in the Trinity. We get a glimpse of this in the blessing and thanksgiving passages found at the beginning of Paul's epistles when he says things like, "Blessed be the *God* and Father of our Lord Jesus Christ."[10] Notice that Paul speaks of the Father as both God and Father of the Lord Jesus. This is not Paul demoting the Son, but rather he recognizes that Jesus was a man. Philippians 2 tells us that Christ humbled himself and took on the form of a man and became obedient even to death. There is a difference between God and man, and this difference

8. 1 Pet. 1:3
9. Jude 1
10. 2 Cor. 1:3; Eph. 1:3; Col. 1:3

is not only in physical and temporal nature, but in hierarchy. Man must be subject to the will of God and only to God. This was what the perfect human nature would understand and do, but when sin entered the nature of man, he became subject in his will to sin and not to God. Jesus, being the perfect man, was not a slave to sin and was therefore only subject to God. To whom, then, was he subject since he was himself God? It was not to a vague sense of God that Jesus was subject to. There had to be a real object of his obedience, and this one was the Father. As Jonathan Edwards says, "God the Father is, in his place, God in such a manner that [he] is not only God to the creature [that is man], but He is God to the other persons of the Trinity in their offices."[11] Jesus acknowledges this himself in John 20:17 when He says to Mary, "Go to My brethren and say to them, 'I am ascending to My Father and your Father, and to My God and your God.'" Edwards's point, though, is that this authority is specifically in his office. By office he means the part each member of the Trinity plays in the plan of God. Recall the concept of the Covenant of Redemption. In this covenant, the Father has taken the role of God, the role of authority.

The Gospel of John is filled with references to the authority of the Father. Over and over again Jesus says that he did not come to do his own will, but the will of his Father, or that he only speaks what the Father taught him.[12] This ultimate expression of submission by the Son to the authority of the Father is found in Christ's prayer in the garden of Gethsemane when he said, "Father, if it is Your will, take this cup from Me; nevertheless, not My will, but Yours be done." There are two things to note in this prayer. First, they were not just words. There is an agony of real meaning in what was going to happen. God had invested that time with reality and importance, so much so that the Son felt it. What is amazing about it is that Jesus knew it had to happen. The events had been prophesied, and from eternity past he knew that this moment would come. This does not diminish the significance of the prayer, of the kneeling on the earth, of the strain and sweat and anguish and terrible anticipation. Second, the Son found it better to do the Father's will than to do his own. He freely gave his obedience, as is indicated elsewhere in John, in that he laid down his own life and no one took it from him. This demonstrates that the obedience was not because the Father was naturally and essentially superior to the Son.[13] If this was the

11. Edwards, "God the Father," 151.
12. John 5:19, 30; 6:38; 7:16–18; 8:28; 10:17–18; 12:49
13. Edwards, "God the Father," 148.

case, then the Son would have had no choice in the matter. But the Son did have a choice. It was the choice of one equal choosing to act according to the will of another equal.

This is difficult to understand, especially having argued that the Son is the communication, the Logos of the Father. Our natural tendency is to assume superiority in quality between the communication and the communicator, and applied to God this would assume superiority in quality the Father over the Son. But authority does not necessarily mean qualitative superiority, especially when the parties are equal. The Son did not cling to equality with God, which indicates something about what the Son perceived about the Father in becoming obedient to him. To the Son, obedience to the Father was something he willingly did, not because the Father could command him, but because the Son loved the Father enough to obey. This same love He passed onto his disciples in teaching them to pray. He said pray in this manner, "Our Father in heaven, hallowed be Your name, Your kingdom come, Your will be done on earth as it is in heaven." It was of such joy to the Son, so much a part of how he saw the universe, that he taught his disciples—then and thousands of years later—to ask for the *Father's* will to be done. There was and is a continuation of authority in the plan of redemption that did not end at the cross, but is still at work.

Again, this is not the kind of authority and submission human beings think about. Normally authority indicates superiority in quality. Countless kings and emperors and governing officials have looked down on the governed because they are the common people—as though there truly was a difference in humanity between the ruler and ruled. The same can be observed in the interaction between different ethnicities. There has been a natural tendency in all ethnicities, at one time or another, to view themselves as superior to all others. But this kind of thinking is driven by sin, and not by perfection and equality. God the Son in eternity past was equal with God the Father, both in quality and station. The change that took place was not a qualitative change, but a station change. The Father, because he is eternally the Father, naturally assumes the role of authority, but this in no way makes him more God than the Son. If both Father and Son are God, then they each possess that quality to its fullest measure. Anything less is not deity in the monotheistic sense. So any authority wielded by the Father is not imposed on the Son. There is no friction in the relationship, which is difficult for humans to grasp.[14] In every relationship we have with other

14. Wilson, "Trinity and Patriarchy" *Sweater Vest Dialogues.*

humans there is friction. In our relationship with God there is friction. But just think if there was no friction! There would be no need for any kind of superiority: superiority in oratory, in power, in skills, anything. The motivating factor would be love. This is the only way for two persons who are eternal and all powerful to enter into an arrangement from eternity past for one to be in authority over the other. And it does exist, for the Father has authority over the Son because that is the way God is.

Inexorably linked to this idea of authority is the concept of organizing and planning. The Father's authority is related to the details of the plan being worked out. That the plan is the Father's plan is expressed in Ephesians 1:5–6 where we are told that God predestined us to "adoption as sons by Jesus Christ to himself, according to the good pleasure of his will, to the glory of His grace, by which He made us accepted in the beloved." Bruce Ware, commenting on Ephesians 1, says, "The Father plans all that occurs, and this plan involves all things being summed up in His very Son."[15] While the Father delegates to the Son the glory and honor of redemption and saving the chosen people, it is the Father who instructs it and orders it.

Ware calls the Father the "Grand Architect" and "Wise Designer" who is organizing all things according to the purpose of God.[16] Architecture and design involve choices of the most intimate detail, and we see such detailed choices expressed in John 6:37–39 where it is written, "All that the Father gives Me will come to Me, and the one who comes to Me I will by no means cast out. For I have come down from heaven not to do My own will, but the will of Him who sent Me. This is the will of the Father who sent Me, that of all He has given Me I should lose nothing, but should raise it up at the last day." This is the kind of design and choice made by God the Father. It is not only his choice that the Son should raise up those who are in Christ, but the Father is the one deciding who is in Christ to begin with. When Paul writes in Galatians 2:20 that "Christ gave Himself for me," he could just as accurately have said, "The Father chose me and gave me to His Son who gave His life for me." The individuals, those who would believe in Christ and be raised up by him, are chosen by the Father.

The Father also chooses to work through the Son and through the Spirit. He sent the Son into the world to save it. He sent the Spirit into the world to sanctify those who are in Christ, prompting those who are saved to cry out, "Abba, Father!" In this way the Son and Spirit have been and are

15. Ware, *Father, Son, and Holy Spirit: Relationships, Roles, and Relevance*, 52.

16. Ware, *Father, Son, and Holy Spirit: Relationships, Roles, and Relevance*, 53

immediately present in the world in a way which the Father is not. To be sure, the Father possesses the quality of God called omnipresence, but there is a difference between this and the idea of location. It is the same difference as was expressed in the dedication of the Tabernacle and the Temple. No tent or building could contain God, and he is already everywhere, but the Bible continually describes an important difference between omnipresence and the resting of God in some particular location. The Son took on flesh and became present in the world, coming to the very temple that was dedicated to his name. The Spirit takes up residence within the temple that is the body of the believer. While Jesus talks about how he and Father will take residence in the disciples by means of the Spirit, there is a still a real sense that the Father did not come into the world. The Son was seen, and in him the Father was seen, but this is not the same as the Father himself being present. No one has seen him, though through the Son they have seen what he is in his fullness. No one has seen him at any time, though the only begotten of the Father has perfectly expressed him.

There is a sense in which the Father is removed from the world, taking on the role of holiness within God. This is not to deny the holiness of the Son or of the Spirit. In Revelation 3:7 Jesus is called holy and true, and the Holy Spirit's name indicates he is holy. But the Father seems to have taken the special role of not interacting directly with the unholy, whereas the Son and Spirit are given the glorious task of doing so. The Father remains unseen by unholy eyes, yet his goal for us is that we actually should be presented to himself as holy and blameless, adopted as sons in his own beloved Son.[17] However, for this to happen, the holiness of God, the holiness kept by the Father, had to be satisfied, and for this reason Christ had to die. The LORD had to lay on him the iniquity of us all.

Often our focus is on what Christ has done in order to bear our iniquities and face the wrath of God. This is a good and proper thing. God has drawn attention to his Son, glorifying him, giving him center stage, and we inevitable focus on the love and anguish of Christ. He took the cup of the wrath of God. At the same time it is important not to lose sight of something: it was the Father who gave the cup to Christ. To truly appreciate the magnitude of what this means, it is necessary to first understand how the Father viewed the Son prior to and during the incarnation.

At the baptism of Jesus, the Father declared that Jesus was his beloved Son, in whom he was well pleased. He said the same thing at the

17. Eph. 1:4–6

transfiguration of Jesus. Paul picks up on this idea in Ephesians 1:6 when he says that we are included in the *Beloved*, meaning Christ. Does Paul mean the *beloved* of men? I think not. Jesus was and is the Beloved of the Father. This was not a love that was hidden from Christ, because Mark and Luke record God saying to Jesus, *"You* are My beloved Son." He spoke directly to Jesus, making it clear that he loved him. Jesus recognized this love, and in John 17:24b he says to the Father, "You loved Me before the foundation of the world." This simple statement opens up the door to the relationship between the Father and Son. The Father loved the Son before creation, before the cross. It was not just a love because Christ obeyed; it was a love for who Christ is.

But these words do not fully relay the actual experience of love had by the Father and the Son. The love which a human father has for his human son is analogous to it. Just as a father loves a son who looks like him or perhaps reminds him of his own character, so too the Father loves the Son because the Son is like him. I do not mean in a physical resemblance, but in nature, thought, desire, ability, and will.[18] These attributes of God are perfect, eminently worthy of being emulated, whereas human thoughts and actions are not always worthy of being passed on. Human love is also temporal: it comes into being at the conception and birth of the child, and it dies when the father dies. The Son has always existed and the Father never dies. The love is eternal, without beginning and end. Far from growing old and stale, the love is ever fresh, ever sweet, because it is everlasting. We cannot really grasp this, but we can try. Jesus invites us to try, and to enjoy this love. He says to the Father, "And I have declared to them [the disciples] Your name, and will declare it, that the love with which You loved Me may be in them, and I in them."[19] This love, which is special between the Father and Son, is so great, so wonderful, that God wants to share it with us!

Now, get a firm grip on this. Yes, look forward to its ultimate fulfillment and revel in it as we currently enjoy it in the Spirit of God. Understand how wonderful it is for us so that you can imagine how much more so it is for the Son and Father. It is a love beyond measure, so unendurably wonderful that God wanted to share it. It is a love that caused the Son to face the cross. Grab hold of that idea and realize what the Father took upon himself to do for our benefit.

18. Edwards, "Discourse on the Trinity," 23–41.
19. John 17:26

When the Father sent the Son to be the Savior of the world, he did not send him to some distant country where the Son could not be reached. The Father could see him and speak to him at all times. When death came it was not a contingency. The Father was carrying out his plan. While in the world, the Son was not beyond the Father's helping. At any moment he could catch the Son up, or smite his enemies. It was not that the Father was a passive observer. When Christ suffered and died it was not because the Father had turned away or that he was helpless to stop it. This is not at all the picture of Isaiah 53. There we are told the Servant—the true, faithful Servant whom we learn is the Beloved Son—was smitten by God and afflicted by him. The *LORD* laid on him the iniquity of us all. Paul says that he who had known no sin became sin for us.[20]

Think of the implications! Habakkuk 1:13 says of God, "Your eyes are too pure to approve evil, and you cannot look on wickedness with favor." If the Son had become *sin* it is not that the Father was forced to look away. This was not the meaning of Habakkuk. God does not turn away in shame or even disgust. His eyes are too pure to look at it and let it go. He will destroy it. Recall the discussion about God's holiness. Sin is attempting to ungod God, and so when he sees it he will punish it. He does not just go away. He pours out his wrath on it because of what it is.

This is the role the Father took. Not only did he send his Son, but he poured out the just punishment for sin upon him.

Just consider the love you might have for your own son or daughter. Think of how you want nothing but the best for them, how all you want is for them to be happy. Now magnify that to such an extent that you can no longer understand it. This is the love of the Father for the Son! All he has ever done from eternity past, as they were face-to-face, was smile at his Son, showering praise, glory, and love upon him. But in that terrible moment, the shining, smiling face burned with indignation. The hand which had blessed the Son and used the Son to make the world—now, in the moment of all moments, that hand smote the Son.

This is the role the Father took.

The Father accepted the sacrifice willingly made by his Son.[21] He accepted the blood of his Son. He poured out the full measure of wrath upon him. Then, to show that he truly does love the Son, he lifted him up, giving him a name that is above every name, that at the name of Jesus every knee

20. 2 Cor. 5:21
21. Heb. 9:14

will bow and every tongue confess that Jesus Christ is Lord to the glory of God the Father! It is to his glory that he brings us all to himself through the Son. He has revealed who he is through the Son, and the Son teaches us that the Father is someone worth knowing. This one who is hidden is worth seeing and knowing. So much so that the Spirit prompts us to call out to him as Daddy! Why would the Spirit do this unless it was worth it?

The Father is, in a sense, the goal for us. He has made us children of God, and children love their father. They want to approach him, to love him, and he in turn wants to be approached, loved, and to love. This is what Paul means in Ephesians 2:18 when, through Christ, in the Spirit, we have access to the Father. We, who were not only strangers to God and his covenants, but were truly his enemies, now have access to him! Paul, in 1 Corinthians 15, talks about Christ defeating death and at the end of all things He will hand the kingdom over to God the Father. What is a kingdom? It is land, laws, and borders, but it is more than that. A kingdom is a people. All of us, all things that belong to Christ the King, are the kingdom, and this is what is handed over to the Father. We are given to the Father at the end of ends! This is something far more intimate, far more precious even than what we have now in the ability to approach the Father in prayer.

The hope of all in Christ is not just Christ. It is through him that our goal lies, for he longs for us to know, love, and experience the love of the Father. Know that if you truly love Christ, then you love the Father and the Father loves you. If you do not love the Father, then you do not love the Son. And if you do not love the Son, you do not love the Father. But if you do love the Son, then embrace what he has done. He has given you access to the Father. The Spirit also works in you to approach the unapproachable. Therefore, direct your prayers to the Father, for this is what Christ has taught his disciples. It is what the Spirit prompts in us when he directs us to cry out, "Daddy!" This is not a neglect of the Son or Spirit. This is what God wants, what the Trinity wants, because the Father is worth it. He is the Originator and the Goal of our redemption. Let us join with Christ our Savior and High Priest to enter the most holy place to approach our God whose mercy is matchless and whose grace is deep. Let us walk in the Spirit with our brother Jesus and approach the Father as our Daddy, whose love is lavish and in whose hands are gifts unimaginable.

7

The Love of God: The Holy Spirit

"Do not cast me away from Your presence,
And do not take Your Holy Spirit from me."

—PSALM 51:11

THERE IS A DOCUMENTARY that I am sure many of you are familiar with. It describes a monumental battle between a band of revolutionaries and an evil, corrupt government. This battle seemed to foretell the end of the revolution, but it proved to be a spark of new hope. At the climax of the battle everything came down to a young man, a farm-boy who through various circumstances found himself in the cockpit of a fighter in the middle of the battle of all battles. It was his job to do what others had failed to do: fire his torpedoes and strike the perfect place to destroy the enemy's base.

His fighter-craft gets closer and closer to the goal. He looks through the special instrument designed to help him hit this target. Then, as he adjusts the instrument, he hears something—a voice perhaps, or maybe it is a memory. It is the voice of his religious teacher, reminding him of a higher power. The voice tells him to let go, and let this higher power work. So the farm-boy lets go. He stops using the instrument—the one thing designed to help him succeed, this he turns off. Moments later he releases his torpedoes.

Well, as some of you probably know, his torpedoes went exactly where they were supposed to go. The Rebel Alliance was saved, the Death Star was destroyed, and Luke Skywalker became a hero.

Now, why do I bring up this story? It is because I think that, as Christians, and as Evangelicals, we have a tendency to view the Holy Spirit a lot like the Force. We talk about the Spirit moving around us in words not too dissimilar to how Obi Wan Kenobi or Yoda might claim the Force is all around everyone in the galaxy. We talk about *feeling* the Spirit like Luke Skywalker might *feel* the Force. We are encouraged to let go and let God (meaning the Spirit), just as Luke was to let go and let the Force.

To compare our understanding of the Holy Spirit with how the Force is portrayed might seem a bit harsh—especially considering how terrible the last three Star Wars movies were—but I don't think it's inaccurate. This is because we have a great deal of uncertainty about who the Spirit is, not only as God, but what makes him different from the Father and the Son. We understand the idea of God the Father on a very basic level because we have all had fathers—whether good or bad. We can deal with God made flesh because people could see the Son, touch him, speak to him, and hear him. But how are we to understand the Spirit? We cannot touch him. We cannot see him. He is like the wind, and perhaps this is the reason we have so much difficulty truly understanding him, and what it means to walk in him and be filled with him.

THE REVELATION OF THE SPIRIT

The Old Testament makes reference to the Spirit of God several times, but it is not until the revelation of the Son of God that the Spirit's full nature comes to light. But while the easiest thing to accept about Jesus is his personhood and the most difficult his divinity, the opposite is true of the Spirit. Few people deny that the Spirit is divine in some sense, but there is a tendency to unperson him.

One could easily put to rest the notion that the Spirit is an impersonal force by turning to Ephesians 4:30. There Paul warns the reader not to "grieve the Holy Spirit of God." Grief is an emotion, a feeling, and proof of personality.[1] As James White puts it, "An impersonal force cannot be grieved, pained, or injured..."[2] Jesus also testifies to the Spirit's personhood when He promises to send another Paraclete (this term will be discussed a little later) to the disciples. He says in John 14:16–17, "I will pray the Father and He will give you another Helper, that He may abide with you

1. Ryrie, *Holy Spirit*, 14.
2. White, *Forgotten Trinity*, 145.

forever—the Spirit of truth..." Jesus does not just say the Father is going to send a Helper, because an impersonal thing can indeed be a great help. A dishwasher is a great helper, so is a computer, and so are those little automatic vacuums that roam around the house on their own—at least I imagine they are helpful. But Jesus does not say the Father is going to send a helper; he says the Father is going to send *another* Helper. The word *another* indicates there was already a Helper with the disciples. Who was this Helper, this Comforter, and Advocate? It was Jesus himself, but Jesus was going away. This other Helper was to take Jesus' place, to be a presence, voice, and comfort. Could any impersonal force fulfill this role that a living person filled? Absolutely not! Does any picture replace the person? No. Likewise, could anyone but God fulfill the role which Jesus fulfilled? Certainly not! But we will come to that in a moment.

The passage in John does more than prove the personhood of the Spirit and hint at his deity. It also differentiates him from the Father and Son. The expression *another* shows that this one replaces Christ in being present with the disciples, and therefore could not be Christ. At the same time the Spirit cannot be the Father because the Spirit is sent by the Father. He must therefore be his own person, distinct from the Father and Son.

This may seem to seal the case for the Spirit's personhood, but in case it does not, consider the following passages found in Acts.

- Acts 5:1–11: This passage tells us the story of the deaths of Ananias and Sapphira. They had sold a possession and kept back part of the proceeds, with the implication being they had promised to give it all. Peter then says, "Ananias, why has Satan filled your heart to lie to the Holy Spirit and keep back part of the price of the land for yourself?" Notice he asks why Ananias lied to the Holy Spirit. You cannot lie to an impersonal force.

- Acts 8:29: Philip, having been directed by an angel to walk along the road from Jerusalem to Gaza, saw a chariot as he walked. The Holy Spirit then said, "Go near and overtake the chariot." This shows the Spirit speaking with a personal voice, giving specific instructions, something an impersonal force cannot do.

- Acts 10:19–20: After Peter had the vision of the sheet filled with animals, when God told him to rise, kill, and eat, three men arrive from Cornelius. The Spirit says to Peter, "Behold, three men are seeking you. Arise, therefore, go down and go with them, doubting nothing for I have sent them." How could anyone but a person say, "I have sent?"

- Acts 13:2–4: There were certain prophets and teachers at Antioch and we are told the Holy Spirit said, "Now separate to Me Barnabas and Saul to the work to which I have called them." Again, only a person can say something like this.

What these last two passages reveal in addition to the Spirit's personhood is that he is God, exercising the authority of God. Who else could command Peter to go with the men from Cornelius "for *I* have sent them," unless that one had the authority to both purpose and send? An angel would have had to say, "Go with these men, for they are sent by God." And who but God could have commanded Paul and Barnabas to be set aside for the work which he had prepared for them? These things, in combination with Jesus' words and Paul's command not to grieve the Spirit, provide the evidence we have to deal with. The Spirit is a person, not an impersonal force.[3] He is differentiated from the Father and Son. At the same time the Spirit is also God in the same, full sense as the Father and the Son.

THE SPIRIT AS THE LOVE OF GOD

When considering what makes the Son unique and different from the Father, we found that in being the Logos he communicates God, and is the express image of him. The Son is the gravitational center of the redemptive work, and the Father has made the entire focus on him. Not so the Holy Spirit. Bruce Ware, in speaking of the Holy Spirit, says, he "does not seek or desire to be the center of attention."[4] James White says this is because it is the "Spirit's role to direct the hearts of men to Christ, and to conform them to his image, He does not seek to push Himself into the forefront and gain attention for Himself."[5] Both Ware and White make the same important point. Though equal with the Father and Son as God, the Spirit chooses not

---

3. In English the implication is then that we cannot refer to the Spirit as *it*. While currently there is a fad that allows and encourages people to choose pronouns that, when properly used, speak of the impersonal (it) or plural (they or them), I do not think humanity is served by thus misusing pronouns. The Spirit is biblically referred to as *him* not because he possesses male equipment, but because he is a person, and he is the Spirit of the Father and Son, both of whom are referred to with male pronouns.

4. Ware, *Father, Son, and Holy Spirit*, 104.

5. White, *Forgotten Trinity*, 139.

to demand the same attention. This is an incredible act of humility on his part, and an amazing expression of unity with the Father and Son. At the same time, however, I think we miss something important if we merely say the Spirit does not want attention. It is the same kind of thing that is missed if we simply say that Jesus does want to be the center of attention.

The reality is that Jesus gets the attention because of who he is in God, not simply that he is God. He is the Logos, the communication, the expression of God. He is the front-man, the figurehead. Likewise the Father is the originator, the one who came up with the plan and directs its execution. It is who he is as the Father. How, then, are we to understand the Holy Spirit? He takes the less visible position, and yet Ware says the Spirit is always assisting the Father in carrying out his work.[6] Indeed, the Spirit is always present in the work God does. Why, then, is the work of redemption to the glory of the Father and Son, but never is it explicitly stated to be to the glory of the Holy Spirit? The answer lies in who the Spirit is, not just in his role. We gain insight from his very name: *Spirit*. The Hebrew terms is *ruwach* and means wind, breath, violent exhalation, mind, spirit, or air. The Greek term *pneuma* carries very similar meanings. That he should be called by this name seems very strange to me, because it is so unlike the ideas conveyed by *Father* and *Son*. We have categories of persons known as father and son, but there is no one in the human family that fits the category of *spirit*.

Things are made more difficult when, in both the Old and New Testaments, various designators are attached to this term *spirit*: holy, truth, Spirit of Yahweh, Spirit of Jesus, the Spirit of adoption, etc. All of these things tell us something about the type of spirit, but it is still difficult to understand. Maybe part of it is that we have so divorced spirit from our daily life. Think about it. We have comparisons between *flesh* and *spirit* where we know what the flesh is but spirit is elusive as the breeze. Then we have the *material* world and the *spiritual* world, living in the former and always in search of the latter—though what exactly we are searching for is difficult to say. Things become even more difficult when we start throwing in phrases such as "being in the Spirit" or "receiving the Spirit" or "walking in the Spirit." For many people the easiest solution has been to make *spirit* synonymous with feelings, so to walk in the Spirit is to *feel* close to God. Unfortunately this does not last very long, and soon we are stuck feeling terrible about ourselves and wondering if we really know God.

6. Ware, *Father, Son, and Holy Spirit*, 105–107.

The first rays of insight concerning the concept of *spirit* came while reading Jonathan Edwards's "Discourse on the Trinity." Edwards points out that in Ephesians 4:23 the apostle tells the reader to be "renewed in the spirit of your mind." The implication in Ephesians is that one can have a renewed or unrenewed spirit of the mind; that is, one can have a renewed or unrenewed temperament or disposition.[7] This is more than an emotion, though certainly emotions are a part of it. It is more like an orientation of the heart or a defining characteristic of the soul. There is an example of this in II Chronicles 18:20–21 where a lying spirit is sent into the mouths of the prophets of Ahab. The disposition of this spirit was deceitfulness. It was what defined him, and it was clearly what he found joy in being. That is the quality that defined him. There is a positive example found in Galatians 4:6 where we read, "And because you are sons, God has sent forth the Spirit of his Son into your hearts, crying out, 'Abba, Father!'" Now this reference to spirit could be understood in two ways. First, it could just be the general mindset of sonship, that is, the mentality by which God the Son cries out, "Abba, Father!" But I find this difficult to believe because in a similar passage found in Romans 8:15–16 we are told that by the Spirit we cry, "Abba, Father!" and this same Spirit is clearly a person because we are told, "The Spirit Himself bears witness with our spirit that we are children of God." Notice the word *himself* which is an indication of personhood. So this Spirit is not just a psychological mindset, but is a person. At the same time spirit *does* carry with it the idea of mindset or disposition, and the Holy Spirit seems to be the embodiment of this particular disposition.

This raises some interesting implications. The Spirit is called the Spirit of the Son. His nature is of sonship, though he is not the Son himself. He is sent into our hearts so that we act as sons and cry out to the Father as such. This seems to indicate that the Spirit is the embodiment of the temperament of God. It is not just of the Son, but of God as a whole, for we should remember that in Galatians it says that God sends the Spirit, and clearly Paul means the Father sends the Spirit. So if the Spirit is given by the Father he must also carry the love of the Father. Think of it this way. A son is not a son by his own power and his own choice. He is a son because he was born as such. It is a father who makes sons in the act of conception or adoption. It is therefore an act of fatherly love to bestow sonship. So too the act of giving the Spirit of sonship is a fatherly act of love on the part of God the Father. Actually, the reciprocal nature of the father-son relationship is

7. Edwards, "Discourse on the Trinity," 30

best defined as love, but a love having two sides. It is like a magnet has two polarities, though it is only one magnet. The Holy Spirit would seem to be the magnet, the love that is shared by both Father and Son, but that love is so perfect, so complete, that he is a person, not merely a feeling.

This idea is borne out in John 17:26. There Jesus says, "And I have declared to them Your name, and will declare it, that the love with which You loved me may be in them and I in them." Notice that the love the Father gives to the Son is the love which Jesus wants to be in the disciples. When they have this love then Jesus will be in them, and the Father too will be with them. How is this to be understood except in the light of Galatians which tells us that the Spirit of the Son is in us? The Spirit, then, is the embodiment of the love of the Father and the Son. The Spirit is the very love of God.[8]

This should not be surprising. First John 4:8 says, "God is love," meaning this is the sum of God's temperament or disposition.[9] But how is this to be understood? It is not a mere emotion or vague sense of kindness and affection. It is the perfect and fullest expression possible—a living love that never dies and is from everlasting to everlasting. If it is eternal, then this love existed before any of us existed, for if God did not love until men were made, then love has not always been a part of his nature. But if love is a part of his eternal nature, as I John would seem to indicate, who did he love? The obvious answer is that the Father loved the Son, for the Father loved the Son before the foundation of the world.[10] It is interesting, though, that we do not read of either the Father or the Son loving the Spirit. Is this because they do not love him? I do not think so. I think it is, as Edwards suggests, that the Spirit is the very love they share.

As perfect, eternal love the Spirit is a person and he is God. This is very similar to the way in which Jesus, as the perfect Logos, is the embodiment of the expression of God. The Son always was, always is, and always will be the image and the expression of the Father. In his perfection he is not just an image or description. He is utterly and completely God. In the same way the Spirit is not just a feeling. He is the eternal and perfect love of God for God, and must therefore be God in his perfection.

Once we have the idea of God eternally loving himself, then we have come back around to the topic of God's holiness and why it is the jewel

8. Augustine *On the Trinity* 15.15.31

9. Edwards, "Discourse on the Trinity," 30.

10. John 17:24

in God's crown. God's zeal for his holiness is ultimately about his love for himself. It is a pure and righteous love, not a divine form of narcissism. So the inescapable unity between divine love and holiness not only exists in theory, but is embodied in the person of the Spirit, for he is called the *Holy Spirit of God*. The divine love is above all separate from all other loves, for it is the only love which forever has been and forever will be. The Father has always loved the Son and the Son has always loved the Father. The love finds perfect expression in reality. Love becomes, for lack of a better term, physical instead of ideal. Both the Father and Son find immeasurable joy in sharing this love with one another—such joy that God wants to share the Spirit with us.

THE SPIRIT IN THE PLAN OF REDEMPTION

When understood as the very Love of God, a great many things about the Spirit fall into place. The Spirit hovers over the waters during creation, and it makes sense that the Love of God might be the empowering motivation behind and within the work. With eagerness he watched and worked as the Father made all things through the Son for the Son. The entire plan for God's grace to be glorified is an act of love for God.

The Spirit is the one who has given the word to the world. By this I mean two things. First, he is the one who has given the scriptures. He breathed out the words, moving the prophets to speak only what he intended.[11] This was an act of love, for even the law teaches what it takes to abide in the presence of God. Second, it was by the Spirit that within the Virgin Mary our Savior was conceived.[12] It is fitting that the Spirit should have done this because, as it says in John 3:16, God "so *loved* the world that He gave His only begotten Son ..." It makes sense that if the Spirit is the Love of God that he would be the one by whom the Son took on flesh.

The Spirit's nature as the Love of God also explains the curious fact that in the Synoptic Gospels Jesus is baptized by the Holy Spirit and then that same Spirit drives Jesus into the wilderness to be tempted. Clearly the descent of the Spirit was the Father expressing his love for his beloved Son. Why, then, would this same Spirit drive Jesus into the wilderness to face the devil—and after fasting for forty days! Was the Spirit suddenly no longer the love of the Father for the Son and the Son for the Father? Certainly not!

11. 2 Tim 3:16 and 2 Pet 1:21
12. Matt 1:18 and Luke 1:35

For what else can Jesus' response to the devil be but an expression of love for the Father? With each reply Jesus gave He was declaring, "I love My Father more than anything you can offer!" The Spirit was the one moving Christ in order for Christ to show love for the Father. The Spirit not only gave Christ the chance to do this, but was the very power by which he stood.

Once we understand the Spirit to be the Love of God, then we understand why he does not seek his own glory. It is because he *is* the glory. His is the very glory in which the Father and Son glory. He is so present in everything going on that the Spirit is the very air of the great story being told. He fills everything so completely that it almost seems like he isn't there. But the Spirit is always present, for the Psalmist says, "Where can I go from Your Spirit, or where can I flee from Your presence?" But the Spirit is not just someone floating around. He convicts the world of sins. He is the one always at work to press the gospel upon our hearts. He is the one whose work is carried out in the book of Acts and his work continues in every tribe, tongue, and nation of the world. He is the very gift being poured out upon us in the New Covenant.

All of this should make it clear why God says that blasphemy against the Holy Spirit is unforgivable. The particular text is Matthew 12:22–37 which tells us that Jesus healed a demon-possessed man who was blind and mute. The Pharisees make the statement, "This fellow does not cast out demons except by Beelzebub, the ruler of demons." Think of that! The Pharisees were saying that the very love of God is the love of the devil. It would be like watching someone get a wonderful Christmas gift and then saying to the gift-giver in all sincerity: "Wow, you hate him!" We would place the emphasis on the *you* in the statement, but that is not what Jesus does. He says that whoever speaks against the Son of Man will be forgiven. It was the idea of *hate* that is unforgivable. The Pharisees at least acknowledged that Jesus was the one casting out the demon! But they said it was by hate, and not by love. So there really is no better word than *blasphemy* to describe this. The Pharisees took what was light and called it darkness. They took perfect Love and said he was wickedly hateful. The very joy of God in himself was the love and joy by which the man's eyes were opened and his tongue loosed. Yet the Pharisees were saying it was not the love of God, but the love of the devil. It was not an overflow of joy but by joy-sucking that the deed was done.

The Pharisees would have said they were zealous for the law of God. They often complained that Jesus healed on the Sabbath, and they wrapped themselves in the law and declared themselves righteous. But what they failed to realize was that the law was and is never about the law. There is a connection between the law and the lawgiver which Jesus makes very clear when he summarizes the law as, "Love the Lord your God with all your heart, soul, mind, and strength." He does not say that all the law is summed up in this: "Obey the law." To say that would be to miss the Spirit. The law does not drive us away from God, and it was never designed to do that. It is by the law that we realize there is sin in our hearts and in our members. What is sin but hatred for God? So the law, when worked upon us by the Holy Spirit, stirs within us the groaning knowledge of who we really are. This is love when we are shown who we really are.

Our culture says that it is love to let people deceive themselves, to think they are something they are not. God's love is different. It is pure. His love is not an abstraction or a mere emotion. His love is a person. And this person shows us in the perfect word of God who we really are and who we should be like. Obeying the law, then, is not what saves us. Obedience is the result of a heart filled with love, the very Love of God.

This is the most wonderful part the Spirit plays in the plan of God. He is the divine nature in which we partake.[13] We get to love God—we who had hated God! Our nature is to shake our fists at God, to try to ungod him, and yet now he gives us the Spirit by which we cry out, Daddy! This is not some undefined love, but something definite, which is exemplified in Christ. He could say, and I think joyfully, "Father, not My will, but Yours be done." But he did not stop there! So many people do stop there, but Jesus did not. After he prayed, He got up to greet those who had come to arrest him. He greeted the betrayer, was unjustly accused, was abused and murdered because of the Spirit that was in him. This is the same kind of Spirit we have been blessed with. It is the Spirit that is in our hearts and flows out joyfully into our actions.

If we walk in the Spirit we will not fulfill the lusts of the flesh, according to Galatians 5:16. A similar statement is found in Romans 8:13 where it says, "For if you live according to the flesh you will die; but if by the Spirit you put to death the deeds of the body, you will live." These are very mysterious statements for those who actually try to understand them. But when the nature of the Spirit is understood as the love of God, then it becomes clear what is meant. If we love God in our life and not just in our words, then we cannot help but avoid the lusts of the flesh. As John Own points

13. 2 Pet 1:4

out, it is the Spirit who puts to death the sin in our bodies, and apart from his work it cannot be done.[14] Everything else that is tried will be in vain. The Spirit must do it, and it must be done in the Spirit. It is mysterious, yes, but not incomprehensible. A disposition that is against God will never fear God. A disposition that loves God cannot sin.

This is the work of the Spirit as the Paraclete (*parakletos* in the Greek), as Jesus calls him in John 14. Different translations will render this word differently: the KJV renders the term *Comforter*, the NKJV has *Helper*, as does the NASB and ESV, while the NIV has *advocate*. Each of these terms seems to touch on some element of the work the Paraclete does, but as an individual descriptors they are inadequate. The work which Jesus describes the Paraclete doing cannot really be described merely as *comfort*: He convicts the world of sin, righteousness, and judgement; he guides the disciples in all truth, telling things to come, glorifying the Son by taking the words of the Son and declaring them to the disciples. *Helper* likewise fails to encapsulate all that this Paraclete does, as does *Advocate*. Would any one of these words describe the fullness of what Jesus did for the disciples while He was with them? Because the Paraclete is *another* Paraclete, and would any single one of these words describe what Jesus did? He comforted at times, he helped at times, but there were times when He "rebuked them for their unbelief, for their sleeping, for having no faith."[15] This is the kind of thing the Spirit does as the Paraclete.

All of this, the rebuking, the advocating, the convicting, and teaching are to get us to live and love God in life. To walk in the Spirit is to set one's mind and orient one's soul to loving God. It is not just that we will want to love God, but that we *do* love him. This is a temperament and a way of life. It is in the moment of temptation asking the very simple question, do I love God? This does not make resisting temptation magically easier, but it does make the choice conscious and clear. Shall you attempt to unseat the one you claim to love? Or will you give up that tempting morsel of sinfulness for the sake of the bond of fellowship with God?

The gift of God in the Spirit is not a fleeting feeling of nearness. The real power and real sign of the Spirit is not in apparent coincidences or some song popping up at the right time. It is the dead man brought to life. It is the hater of God turned into the lover of God. It is a love springing out of the deep well of the heart and flowing to the lips and limbs and beyond in

14. Owen, *Mortification of Sin in Believers*, 57–59.

15. Dixon, "Other Comforter: The Place of the Holy Spirit in the Trinity", 96.

the exercising of the gifts given by the Spirit for the church. It is expressing the worth of God in spirit and truth, in confessing all that is good and holy, and in obeying all that is good and holy. It is love, joy, peace, patience, kindness, goodness, faithfulness, gentleness, and self-control; in a word, it is the law of God. It is love. It is the love expressed for the brethren, for those who are in Christ no matter your skin color, no matter your sex, no matter your economic or political position, no matter your social status. It is true love and true fellowship that displays itself in speaking to one another, in eating with one another, in sharing with one another, in working together, in suffering together. The wonderful reality of the Spirit is that he does this for people from such diverse backgrounds, who would otherwise have nothing to do with one another. He says to them, "Take part in Me, have fellowship with others like you, and have fellowship with the Father and Son."[16]

One could say, quite accurately, that all of this is obedience to the law of God, and that if we are in the Spirit then we would want to obey the law. As it is written, "If you love Me, keep My commandments."[17] And again he says, "By this all will know that you are My disciples, if you have love for one another."[18] Love for God and love for the brethren is the summation of the law of God. It is the law by which God lives, for he loves himself, as demonstrated in the Father's love for the Son and the Son's love for the Father. This flows outward, as the second command to love one's neighbor flows out of love for God. God does love those who are not himself. He loves some enough to save them. Those who do not come to him get a benefit of love. That is, they are the recipients of love for God in their state: they receive justice. When he judges them it will be fair and impartial, and when God commands us to love our neighbors, we also give fellowship-love to those who share the same Spirit, but those who do not share the Spirit we must show justice because of our love for God.

This love for God is what we have been given in the Spirit. It is real love, it is expressed, it is identifiable, and is lived. When understood this way, it offers clarity to Hebrews 6:4–6 where we are told that there are people who partake of the Holy Spirit but fall away. These people actually do partake of the Spirit, but in the sense just described. They have enjoyed the love of

---

16. This seems to be the implication of the Spirit's words in 1 John; the entire intent of the letter being that we should abide in the Spirit, abide in the love of God so that we might have fellowship with the Father, the Son, and with one another, and so that our joy might be full.

17. John 15:17.

18. John 13:35.

the brethren, which is the Spirit. So this is what I think the author means by saying they have partaken of the Holy Spirit. It does not mean that the Spirit took up residence in these peoples' hearts as the temple of God, but that they enjoyed the benefits of the Spirit lived out. There have always been people who have benefited from the Spirit working in God's people who were not themselves God's people.

Those of us who have received the Spirit have received a wonderful gift: God himself. We get to share in him in a mystical and yet real way. It is the mystery of the sinner's stony heart turned to flesh so that every beat is for the love of God. It is not ethereal. It is not unknowable. It is as tangible as men and women of every skin color and tongue helping one another. It is as knowable as a slave being treated as a brother. It is as has hard as saying "Father, not my will but Yours be done" and then actually acting upon it. But this obedience is not a burden, because the Father is worth obeying. The Son is worth obeying. It is a joy to get to love God. It is the joy of obeying the Spirit, of partaking of him, and getting to love God. If someone turns away, what other hope, what other joy is there to be found? God is giving us that which has eternally defined him, and in which he finds such joy. If we reject that, what more does he have to offer but wrath?

It seems to me that all the laws of the Old Testament, all the prophesies, all the judgements, the gospel message, and the commands of Christ are wrapped up in who the Spirit is. If only we recognize this, then I think we will embrace those things God has given us to do. I do not just mean the special things, such as should I take this job or that, or the special roles of apostles, prophets, teachers, or any other gift. I mean the very general things given to all disciples: those things given to men and women, to children, to masters and slaves. I mean those things given to elders, deacons, and to the flock. I mean all those things having to do with life—as boring and as tedious as it can be. It is controlling the tongue, bearing with one another, forgiving one another, younger people respecting older people, men and women obeying the rules of the household. All of these things are the direction God gives us in the Spirit. We walk in the Spirit when we follow what he has directed in his scriptures. When he becomes the breath of our lives and the temperament of our souls, then will we be having a little taste of the eternal joy set before us. For when we abide in him, fellowshipping properly with one another, then truly our fellowship is with God the Father and with his Son through the Holy Spirit. Amen.

8

The Accusing Parlor

"You see . . . at first I thought the Anthropomorphic Problem—the fact that we can only conceive of extraterrestrial life as basically human—I thought it was a failure of imagination. Man is man, all he knows is man, and all he can think of is what he knows. Yet, as you can see, that's not true. We can think of plenty of other things. But we don't. So there must be another reason why we only conceive of extraterrestrials as humans. And I think the answer is that we are, in reality, terrible frail animals."

—MICHAEL CRICHTON[1]

HERCULE POIROT AND NERO Wolfe mysteries often seem to end in everyone involved in the story being drawn together into a single room where the detective unravels the mystery. Whether it was the little Belgian detective methodically moving from person to person with his mustache quivering, or the seventh-of-a-ton detective seated in his yellow chair barking at people, they both would tie everything neatly together. Frequently this would involve appearing to accuse different people, building the tension until at last revealing the guilty party. What is interesting is that the detective rarely saw the crime happen. He may know some or all of the general facts, but his words are interpretations rather than a mere regurgitation of facts. Why did they interpret? Because the facts themselves needed interpreting! They needed to be understood and communicated.

1. Crichton, *Sphere*, 118

The reason I begin this way is because many critics of Trinitarianism will point out that the term *Trinity* is not found in the Bible. Such accusations are, of course, completely accurate, but this does not mean the concept is erroneous any more than the lack of the term *Bible* in the Bible makes its use erroneous. What the concept *Trinity* attempts to describe is what the apostles experienced and the biblical writers bear witness to. It is a conclusion derived from the evidence, and this is one of the more exciting things about this doctrine. It is like a mystery and we are the detectives. We are presented with evidence and we need to figure out what the evidence means.

Of course, since the conclusion is derived it means that there will be many interpretations of the evidence. This does not mean that each interpretation is valid, but we must accept that there *are* other interpretations. It is important to recognize this and be able to explain why only one interpretation (or none) is correct while the others are incorrect. Unfortunately, too many people focus solely on the latter part of this, why other opinions are incorrect, without ever really doing the work of summarizing what the correct stance is. This is the purpose of this chapter. Here the evidence which has been presented so far will be brought together into a coherent whole. When this is done, and all the data is accounted for, then we must necessarily come to the orthodox conclusion: that there is one God in three persons.

What you will find in trying to bring everything together is that there are particular words that must be carefully defined. If nothing else, this chapter should demonstrate the importance of defining words. This has application in all areas of life, and our culture would be in a much better shape if we would just learn the discipline of definition.

To begin, it is first necessary to refresh ourselves on the evidence. There are two main concepts. The first is that there is only one God. He is living and active, the creator and sustainer of all things. This is the foundation upon which the Christian confession stands. Christians are absolute monotheists, meaning we do not believe there was, is, or ever will be another God. This is the witness of scripture: "Before Me there was no God formed, nor shall there be after Me."[2]

It is important that this be clear. Christians are *absolute* monotheists, and we must be careful with our language at this point, especially when interacting with other faiths, such as Islam. An article on the Crossway website illustrates this in a negative way. There, in distinguishing between

2. Isa. 43:10

Christian monotheism and Islamic monotheism, Dr. Timothy Tennent states, "Islam teaches a doctrine of absolute monotheism known as *tawhid*. Absolute monotheism is distinct from the *Trinitarian* monotheism of Christianity in that the Qur'an permits no distinction within God."[3] Notice the differentiation is between *absolute* monotheism and *Trinitarian* monotheism. Just think about that for a moment. What is the opposite of *absolute*? Probably it would be something like *imperfect* or *incomplete*. Anything that is *absolute* is the real deal. You either tell the absolute truth or you tell the truth diluted by a lie, and a truth so diluted becomes a lie. When discussing monotheism, by comparing absolute and Trinitarianism in this way, it is difficult to argue against the Qur'an when it says "do not say 'three'—stop [this], that is better for you—God is only one God . . ."[4] For what kind of defense could be offered if Christians said, well, no, we're not absolute monotheists?

The question must be does the Bible teach something different than what the Qur'an says? Think carefully about this question. The Qur'an teaches there is absolutely only one God. Does the Trinitarian doctrine say there is not absolutely one God, but that there are three Gods? That is the assumption made in the *sura* quoted, but it is not a true assumption. It is an assumption one could draw by hearing a Christian contrast *absolute* and *Trinitarian*, but it is a misunderstanding. The Christian doctrine is founded unequivocally on the idea of *one,* not on the idea of *three.* The entire teaching of the Old Testament—indeed the very history of the nation of Israel—drives this point home. Just consider what occurred in Israel's history. The nation was commanded to serve the one God and was told time and again that there is only one God and all the gods of the other nations were but idols—things made by human hands out of wood, stone, or metal. Yet Israel did not hold onto this truth, and it took the Babylonian exile to finally purge other gods from their worldview. Had you run across an Israelite in the era of the kings he might just as well have worshiped Ba'al as Yahweh, and might even have worshiped both. Meet an Israelite now and without a doubt he will worship one God or no gods. The defining trait of the Israelites before the Exile was not monotheism, but it certainly has been ever after. And the Christian church has inherited this truth of monotheism.

True monotheism is the first bit of evidence the Bible presents. The second is that the Bible tells us there is someone named the Father,

---

3. Tennent, "The Bible and Islams."
4. Qur'an 4:171

someone named the Son, and someone else named the Holy Spirit. Each of these three is either directly identified as the one God Yahweh or else acts as that one God, claiming to have the authority of God. This evidence requires careful consideration because it is in trying to reconcile the existence of these three with monotheism that has gotten people in trouble over the centuries.

One interpretation that comes up regularly in Church history is that Jesus is not really God. Any authority Jesus had was derived authority: the kind of authority a messenger might have, or a king's servant might wield. It is the authority of a prophet, for just consider what Yahweh said of the re-lationship between Moses and Aaron, "you shall be to him as God."[5] While it is one thing for a man to speak with the authority of God, and to act with all the conviction of a true prophet, it is another thing entirely to receive worship. Yet this is exactly what Jesus did. Prophets and angels have no right to receive worship, and they would blaspheme if they did. So if Jesus was merely a prophet, or even if he was an angel, he should have stopped those bowing down to him, even as an angel did twice in the book of Rev-elation when John fell down at his feet. Both times the angel said, "See that you do not do that!"[6] But when men fell at the feet of Jesus He accepted it.[7] Even when John fell at his feet and Jesus laid his hand on him, it was not to forbid worship; it was merely to say, "Do not be afraid; I am the First and the Last."[8] This is an echo of Isaiah 44:6 where Yahweh says, "I am the First and the Last; besides Me there is no God."

The Bible offers no room for the option that Jesus was merely a prophet, or merely a servant. The only way to make such a suggestion is to conclude that the text of the New Testament has been corrupted by insert-ing sections where Jesus is worshiped. This corruption must have been so early and so skillfully done that these sections fit seamlessly with the sur-rounding texts. But this is really only an option for the non-Christian bent on denying not only the deity of Christ, but also the textual history of the New Testament. So we must reject this concept of Jesus, for the Bible clearly teaches he is God.

Of course, there have been those in history who have acknowledged this and yet not arrived at the orthodox position. One of the most important

5. Exod 4:16.
6. Rev 19:10 and 22:9.
7. Matt 2:11; 14:33; 28:9.
8. Rev 1:17.

examples of this is what has been labeled Modalistic Monarchianism or Sabellianism. The basic idea is that the one God expressed or revealed himself in different modes of activity.[9] There is only one someone, and that someone is God. Father, Son, and Spirit are just masks and there is really no distinction between the members of the Godhead. The ancient teacher of a form of this doctrine, Sabellius, is said to have called the Godhead "Son-Father" in order to make clear that there really is no difference within God.[10] With no clear distinction then it was not just the Son who suffered on the cross but the Father also, for the two are one and the same in this perspective. This concept came to be known as Patripassianism, meaning *Father suffering*.

Modalism presents Father, Son, and Spirit not as *whos* but as *whats*. The trouble with this is obvious when two things are considered. First, the Son and Spirit have conscious personalities that are other than the Father. This is especially clear in the way Jesus speaks of the Father. He says, "I" and "me" and speaks of the Father as "Father" or as "He." Some*one* not some*thing* says things like this. And the love and intimacy with which he addresses the Father is of such a nature that he must be speaking of and to someone else. And the same is true of the Father. Both at Christ's baptism and his transfiguration the Father says, "This is My beloved Son . . ." Are we really to believe that God ran upstairs quick to speak as the heavenly voice and then ran downstairs to act and speak as the Son? What would be the point? But what makes it all the more difficult is at the mountain the Father not only says that this is his Son, but he then commands, "Hear Him!" Here we have one someone saying to a group of someones to heed the words of still another someone. Finally there is John 12:28 which has Jesus saying, "'Father, glorify Your name.' Then a voice came from heaven, saying, 'I have both glorified it and will glorify it again.'" So once again we have two *whos* speaking to one another.

It is obvious that the scriptural evidence does not support the idea that Father, Son, and Spirit are masks God wears. There is something deeper, more complex going on, and we are forced to come to a different theory. There is one God and yet three *whos* identified as God. So it is necessary first to understand what we mean by there being one God.

One of the clearest passages where the three identify with one is found in Matthew 28:19. There Jesus commands that his disciples be baptized in

9. Ferguson, *Church History Volume I*, 143.
10. Gonzalez, *History of Christian Thought Volume I*, 145.

the name of the Father, and of the Son, and of the Holy Spirit. Notice he does not say the *names* of the Father, Son, and Spirit. He also does not say, "in the name of the Father, and the name of the Son, and the name of the Spirit" as though dunking three times for three different names. Instead Jesus commands baptism in the singular name which all three share. The Father identifies with the name. The Son identifies with the name. And the Spirit identifies with the same name. They each possess it equally and completely. It is not a coat passed from one to another, and there is only one name it could possibly be that these three share: Yahweh.

This is more than the sharing of a name, because this name is sacred and holy. It is *the* name and it is the kind of name humans cannot possess. Oh sure there are names like Isaiah (Yahweh is salvation), Jeremiah (Yahweh will raise), or Obadiah (servant of Yahweh), but in these instances the name has taken hold of the person, to change him into a statement about Yahweh or the person's relationship to him. But the name itself is possessed by no normal man. Only Yahweh can truly and in the fullest sense be Yahweh. In this way, though this is God's name, it is also so unique and so powerful that it contains the very essence of monotheism. There is only one Yahweh because there is only one I AM. There is, therefore, only one self-existent and all powerful being. There is only one God. There is such a connection between the two that to speak of Yahweh is to speak of the one God, and to speak of the one God is to speak of Yahweh. But while the two are intertwined with one another in an inseparable way, they do convey two separate ideas.

Just think of it this way. Suppose there is a man named John. If John was in a group of people, a group of human beings, and you wanted to get his attention, by what designation would you call him? Would you say, "Hey, human!" Or would you say, "Hey, man!" Neither of those would work because John is a human, as is everyone else in the room, and unless he is the only male, then *man* only narrows down the possible people by half. One must call him by his name if you want to get his attention. Now let's suppose John found himself beamed off earth by a band of marauding Klingons and whisked away to a penal asteroid. He finds himself placed in a prison filled with Vulcans, Andorians, Gorn and Bajorans. Strangely, he is the only human in the place. So when the Klingon guard shows up and barks, "Human, come here!" everyone knows exactly who is being addressed. Now if Captain Kirk, Mr. Scott, or Dr. McCoy were in the prison with John, then there would be some difficulty figuring out who the Klingon was talking to.

Why? Because *human* is not a name as much as it is a descriptor of being or of a nature. By saying, "Human, come here!" the Klingon is actually saying, "You who have the qualities and characteristics that make you a human and not something else . . ."

There is a term that is usually linked with *human* and that is *being*. If *human* denotes specific qualities which make one thing a particular thing and not another thing, then *being* is the general category of thing. In this way everything has being. Cats have being in that they have a holistic quality, substance, or essence which makes a cat a cat and not a dog. Rocks have being in that they possess a quality which makes them rocks and not bread—such as flying through glass and not being digestible. So too Yahweh possesses a particular essence and quality which makes him one thing and not another. That essence, that quality is God. He is a God-being. Actually, He is *the* God being. There are multiple human beings that differ from one another. On a very basic level there are two types of human beings: male and female. Not so with God. There are not multiple God beings. The Bible is adamant. There is only one God.

The being of God has many elements. He is of course, holy, all powerful, all knowing, everywhere, and eternal. There is another quality that is a part of God, and that is personhood. Rocks do not possess personhood. We speak of a rock as *it*, and rocks speak of themselves as, well, nothing at all. We speak of one another as he, she, you, us, or them. This is not just recognizing sexual traits; it is recognizing personhood. Part of what makes us human is personhood. Our humanity is not what makes us different from other humans; it is who we are as a person that makes us different. At one level this may be sexuality, but this only differentiates us from half of humanity. What marks us as individuals, as unique persons, are a complex array of physical traits, bio-chemical processes, experiences, moods, desires, hopes, and dreams.Our humanity is the *what* which we share with all other humans. Our personhood is the *who* which we share with no one. The distinction between these two concepts is vital in understanding the biblical revelation. When we are told there is one God it would be like saying there is only one human. There is only one being who possesses the qualities of God. There are not three. There is only one. The startling thing that the biblical evidence presents is that there are three *whos* even in this singular *what*.

This is probably the most alien thing about God, because the Bible is not teaching that there are three personalities that flick on and off in God as though he had what used to be called multiple personalities disorder. No, the Father, Son, and Spirit are always alive, always awake and active. They even relate consciously to one another. This kind of thing is strange and alien to us because we do not experience it, but just because we do not experience it ourselves does not make it illogical. We humans would acknowledge that cats have a certain personality, but none of us has ever been a cat. We can read human emotions into a cat, but we can never actually know and experience what it is like to be a cat. Nevertheless, we accept cats in their irritatingly cattish ways.

Science fiction writers have, whether they know it or will admit it, provided valuable theological input when they attempt to express the alienness of aliens. These authors, and most of their readers, accept the otherness of aliens if aliens exist. Michael Crichton in his book *Sphere* lists all sorts of ways aliens can be different. They might breathe in air and exhale some kind of gas that would instantly kill humans. They might not see in colors and shapes, but might have sound or feeling as the primary senses. Aliens might exist primarily in the fourth dimension and so be invisible to us because we only experience things visibly in three dimensions. All of these things are plausible because aliens are not human, and developed in a different environment with a different history. The point Crichton makes is that non-humans are not humans. So why, then, is it so difficult and illogical to say that there are three persons that make up the one God? Just because our experience is one being = one person this does not mean it is illogical to describe God as one being = three persons.

There are some people who will ask, isn't this impossible? The answer is that it is only as impossible as an eternal, omniscient, omnipotent, and omnipresent being. Once you allow for there to be such a being as God, then upon what basis can you say God cannot be Triune? Yet there are those who insist that Trinitarian doctrine is tantamount to polytheism. Such an insistence is based on a conflation of *being* and *person*. But when we allow these things to mean in theology what they mean in daily life, then we find that, though they are related, they are not the same. One describes the *what* and the other the *who*.

While all of this might seems rather strange, it is what the biblical data presents us with. The strangeness of it is irrelevant to the discussion. The use of words such as *being* and *person* do not invalidate the conclusion because they are attempts to understand and express the evidence. It is like the detective gathering everyone together in the accusing parlor. He does not have a recording of what happened that he can play on a screen. Instead he has the evidence. He has the dead body, the scene, and the circumstance. Finally, he has his mind. When he lays out his conclusions it is in his words and yet it aligns with the reality of the evidence. This is what we too must do in examining and wrestling with the biblical evidence.

So what is the solution to our mystery? Over the centuries there have been different formulations. One of the more detailed is the Athanasian Creed, which was written sometime in the fifth or sixth centuries.

> And the Catholic Faith is this: That we worship one God in Trinity, and Trinity in Unity; Neither confounding the Persons: nor dividing the Substance [Essence]. For there is one Person of the Father: another of the Son: and another of the Holy Ghost. But the Godhead of the Father, of the Son, and of the Holy Ghost, is all one: the Glory equal, the Majesty coeternal. Such as the Father is; such is the Son; and such is the Holy Ghost. The Father uncreated: the Son uncreated: and the Holy Ghost uncreated. The Father incomprehensible [unlimited]: the Son incomprehensible [unlimited]: and the Holy Ghost incomprehensible [unlimited, or infinite]. As also there are not three uncreated: nor three incomprehensible [infinites], but one uncreated: and one incomprehensible [infinite]. So likewise the Father is Almighty: the Son Almighty: and the Holy Ghost Almighty. And yet they are not three Almighties: but one Almighty. So the Father is God: the Son is God: and the Holy Ghost is God. And yet they are not three Gods: but one God... So there is one Father, not three Fathers: one Son, not three Sons: one Holy Ghost, not three Holy Ghost...He therefore that will be saved, must [let him] thus think of the Trinity.[11]

The author or authors of this creed had thought through the evidence in detail, listing not only what the Trinity is, but also what it is not. A more succinct explanation of the Trinity is offered by James White who summarizes it this way: "Within the one Being that is God, there exists eternally coequal and coeternal persons, namely, the Father, Son, and Holy Spirit."[12] This, then, is the explanation of the mystery. It is the interpretation that best fits the data, but why does it matter? Why does the Athanasian Creed go into such detail, and why does White write an entire book on the subject? Why is this doctrine of God so important?

11. "Athanasian Creed," 66–71.
12. White, *Forgotten Trinity*, 26.

The Athanasian Creed is explicit: "He therefore that will be saved must thus think of the Trinity." White would likewise see Trinitarianism as necessary to salvation and would quote John 8:24 to prove the point: "For if you do not believe that I am *He*, you will die in your sins." And these are not just two extreme perspectives on the subject. To the Christian church, belief in the Trinity has been fundamental to what it means to have a right relationship with God. But why the emphasis on the *Trinity*? Jesus is not saying in John that unless you believe in the doctrine of the Trinity you will die in your sins. He is saying you must believe he is Yahweh or you will die in your sins. How can one go from believing Jesus is God to requiring belief in the Trinity?

Part of the trouble is that doctrines are viewed rather like math problems. Few people like math problems, and those that do are generally boring or deeply troubled people. It is the common complaint of high school and college students that in the real world they will never use the math they are learning. So too the doctrine of the Trinity is seen as something required of the faith, a sort of prerequisite to being called orthodox, rather like there are prerequisite classes before getting to the really enjoyable college classes. What this perspective fails to appreciate is that God is not a college course. God is not merely a faith. He is a being. He is revealed in persons. To ignore what he reveals about his very nature would be like ignoring some intimate and foundational part of your spouse's nature. Wives, if your husband failed to treat you as a woman, in all that it means, what would be the status of your relationship? Men, if your wives failed to affirm your nature as a man, how would you feel about your wife? Or take a broader example. What does it mean to treat someone like a human being? It is to recognize and appreciate his or her physical nature as well as their mental and emotional natures. Why do we think God would be any less frustrated if we refused to acknowledge his nature?

God is not an equation; he is a being. He is a being that includes not only such things as omniscience, omnipotence, and omnipresence. He is a being who has conscious persons: who love and are loved. God has emotions. He knows himself and wants to be known by us. This is why he has revealed his Trinitarian nature. To ignore this revelation, to make it insignificant, would be like ignoring a human's body or personhood. It would be to treat a human as other than human. In the same way, when we fail to appreciate God as Three-in-One we fail to treat him as God. Divinity is not simply being other than and higher than human. It is to have a certain set of unique characteristics. To truly know him, is to appreciate what makes him unique. The Trinity, more than anything else, makes God unique, makes him beautiful, and if we love him, then we will appreciate this beauty. To ignore it, or the reject it, is to reject who and what he is.

This is why the doctrine of the Trinity is so important. This is what makes unraveling the mystery so worthwhile, and like other mysteries this is not the end. Whenever Poirot or Wolfe revealed who it was that committed the crime, the work was not over. The culprit had to be dealt with, a trial conducted, and judgement rendered. In the same way our work with the doctrine of the Trinity is not ended with its basic formulation. There are ramifications for God's nature, not only for how we relate to God, but also how we are to live. The following chapters offer suggestions for how our knowledge of God's nature should impact our lives.

9

Let All Things Be For Edification

"The first church devoted itself to the community. It was inconceivable
that anyone would not be vitally involved in the life of the local church."

—Jeff Reed[1]

MANY CHRISTIANS FIND THEOLOGICAL studies and discussions to be off-
putting because they too often go nowhere and are useless unless someone
happens to dust off a copy of *Bible Trivia.* The study of God's Trinitarian
nature is no different. It is perceived, more often than not, as something
that is primarily believed or assented to. Churches comment on it in their
doctrinal statements—a thing which the members of the church affirm
with about as much conviction as they affirm the existence of a salad bar
at a buffet. The salad is there, and some people take from it almost in an
obligatory way, but it is primarily there for conscience's sake, and for a few
health-conscious people whom the rest of us wish would just eat some-
where else. And, unfortunately, this is the how the doctrine is taught. It is a
theological category of orthodoxy that exists, but is rarely used.

What is needed is for the local church to be reengaged with the study
of God. More than this, teachers of theology need to present their work in
such a way that benefits the *life* of local assemblies. It must be recognized
that it is the church, the local church, which is the pillar and support of the
truth. Therefore teachings such as the doctrine of the Trinity must become

---

1. Reed, *Paradigm Papers,* 273.

what it really is: an idea, because ideas are infectious and driving. The doctrine of the Trinity as it is popularly perceived is not infectious or driving; it is stale and still. This is not God's fault. It may well be the fault of the teaching itself, or the perception of the teaching. It is therefore my purpose in this chapter to show how an understanding of the Trinity can, should, and does affect our relationship with God, our individual lives, and the lives of our local churches.

RELATIONSHIP TO GOD

The first and most important way in which the doctrine of the Trinity is to inform our lives is in our relationship to God. All of history, which is all of redemptive history, is only understandable from the Trinitarian perspective. As we have seen, the Father is, in a sense, the Holy of holies. He is the One no one but the Son has seen. There is something deeply special about him; not that he is more God than the Son or Spirit. No, it is like he is the special wine which is usually served at the beginning of the feast, but that the Son has reserved until the end of the age. But God is not just reserved. He is reserved in holiness, but not a holiness that is dark like some ancient pagan god hidden in shadows. The Father's holiness is unapproachable light. This unapproachableness is not because he is undesirable, but because he is ultimately desirable.

All of theology is bent upon knowing this one who is so above us and so unapproachable that at times we forget he is there. This is the wonder and the mystery of true deity. It is the kind of thing that makes religion something beyond science and which makes every science a religion. It is the quest for the great unseen—that hidden something or someone which drives every scientific discovery and every mystery cult. It is the unseen God who haunted the ancients, causing them to tremble in fear that at any moment they might be struck dead, and also to tremble at the thought that they might, just for a moment, get a true glimpse of God. Every prayer, every nightmare, every ounce of hatred, and every hope of love are motivated by this.

There was and is a fear associated with knowing or seeing God—a fear which never seemed to go away when certain Old Testament people saw God and yet lived. Seeing God never lessened the idea. It is not like air travel, which had been dreamed of by so many writers and thinkers over the centuries, but is now so ordinary that millions of people do it every year.

If anything, God seemed to grow more holy, more reserved and distant as time went by. When the ancient heathens felt their gods dying, slowly but inevitably turning to myths and plays and Disney movies, there remained a feeling that God was there behind the stories and frivolity.

Today we experience the same thing. God is unseen. We cannot feel him as if he was some kind of goose-bumpily feeling. There is something about him that is too holy for eyes to see or ears to hear, and we especially feel this if we have an accurate understanding of ourselves. A true gaze into the well of the soul reveals dark waters, frothy and oily if only we really look. But God! Oh, but God must be lofty! He must be good and perfect, and so high, so very high above us!

What the revelation of the Trinity teaches us is that God's nature accounts for all of this, and affirms it. God *is* the desirable one. To know him would be to know the best kept treasure in the universe—beyond the universe, really. To speak to him would silence every question and at the same time enflame even the calmest soul. Yet he is hidden, unseen, and absolutely holy.

What is so beautiful about the revelation of the Trinity is that this same one who is so unapproachable, the exalted, the unbearably bright and pure, the Holy One is the same one who originates redemption, salvation, and reconciliation. It is the Father's will being done in redemption; it is his plan and purpose being executed. Within his person he holds perfectly these two things: holiness and graciousness. That the Father would preserve the holiness of God and yet would be drawing men to himself through Christ should fill us with love and awe. Too often we consider holiness to be a withdrawing from the world, a turning in on one's self or one's church in an introverted way. It is very difficult to think of preserving anything of such immense worth any other way. Collectors do it with treasures, misers with their gold, and parents with their children. They hide them away, keeping the world out so as to preserve the sanctity and value of the hidden one. Within his person the Father does this, and yet he also is sharing it with those he chooses.

He wants and will let others enjoy this holiness, but it comes at a price. To perfectly accomplish preservation and sharing, sin must be dealt with. Even atheists know this. When they complain about the world being such a bad place that surely God does not exist, what they are really saying is that the world is such a bad place it is no wonder God does not dwell among men. Yet there must be some way of showing the Father to people, to reveal his values and his ways, and make a way to come to him. Who better to do this than the one who is the perfect image of the Father? Who but the Son could reveal the immense worth of the Father? Who but the Son could communicate him? Who but the Son should enter the world to serve as Priest and Sacrifice, not only communicating God but making a way for man to commune with God? And this the Son did. He did it so well that He includes us in himself so that we might call the Father our Father.

This is the wonderful unity we have in Christ. When the Father looks at us he does not see the enemies we were; he sees his beloved Son. We have become so much a part of him that to reject us would be like one of us rejecting an arm or a leg—except infinitely more so! A father might reject the person of a rebellious son, but what father would reject a son who is his perfect image, always loving and obedient in all things? No good father would do this, and the love the Father has for his Beloved Son is far, far greater than this. And we are included in his Son!

There is little wonder then that Paul described Christ's love for the church and our unity with him in terms of marriage.[2] There is a union between husband and wife that is intimate, that really cannot be described. But there is also an inheritance of love which the wife receives—or there ought to be. It is the inheritance that she does not need to speak of her father-in-law as *father-in-law* but can simply call him *dad*. She is given, by virtue of marriage to his son, full access to the father-in-law so that *in-law* is not a barrier but an invitation and expression of certainty. This is exactly what we get to experience. By virtue of the law's fulfillment in the Son we are joined with him and get to approach the Father in the same way he does: as Daddy.

Think of it! The great mystery of deity, of God unapproachable, is fulfilled! It is not done away with. The wonder and mystery of it are still there, but the fulfillment of the mystery is its discovery. That is true for any good mystery story, because a good mystery story does not become a bad one once the end is reached. A good mystery is still a good mystery, and is especially so when you know the end of it. An excellent example of this is G.K. Chesterton's story "The Blue Cross." Even knowing what is going on and how it ends does not detract from the journey and the clues. If anything it makes it even better because now it is not just about getting to solve the mystery, but to appreciate what the writer has done. And the same is true when at last we are presented to the Father. The enjoyment will not

2. Eph 5:31–32.

only remain, but will be magnified. The wonder never goes away because it never grows old.

But a realistic examination of the human heart will reveal that no one seeks after God, and so no one would go through the door that is Christ. It is probably because what lies through the door is not some small room with a little treasure that can be picked up. Rather, the door opens onto the vastness of the eternal God who cannot be grabbed hold of and carried away. Because we cannot snatch him up and control him, we despise him. We wish for ways to bring him down to manipulate him. We have an anti-spirit who refuses to acknowledge God and his commands. This is evident even in the churches that profess Christ as Lord, for even there we find the divine law ignored, glossed over in the name of love. So it is deep down inside of us, this sin and desire to ungod God. It is so deep down that often we cannot see it even when we look for it. And this is the problem. Because if we will not approach the Father of lights even by means of the Door who is the Son, how then shall we enter at all?

This is exactly the part the Spirit plays. He is the one by whom the Father draws anyone to the Son. He is the one who works in our hearts, prompting us not only to seek God as God, but who convinces our souls that we are children of God and can cry out to him as Daddy. The Spirit is the one sanctifying us, causing us to love God all the more so that when we call him our Father it carries with it all the weight of truth, experience, and boldness.

The Spirit is the very gift of God. He is the love of God, and if we partake in him we partake in fellowship with God. But the Spirit has been given as a down payment. And what kind of down payment is this? For God has given us God, not once but twice: first in the person and work of the Son, and now in the person and work of the Spirit. What more could we ask for? What more could there be? But there is more! Consider this, we have been given the Son and the Spirit, the one side-by-side and face-to-face with men, and the other dwelling within us. Only the Father remains, and what a glory at last we shall see!

All of this is what God has chosen to do. Each member, containing the fullness of God, chose to do this. It is how he has chosen for us to interact with him. None of us reach the Father except through the Son. You cannot reach the Father by the Spirit because unless we are clothed in Christ then the Spirit will not have been working in us. Or if we think our goal is the Spirit then we have missed the work of the Spirit, for he causes us to love

Christ and to love the Father. If we think our goal is Christ then we will miss the whole reason for his sacrifice. It is not just so that we might avoid wrath, as if by avoiding wrath we achieve a neutral state with God. No, it was to cause the veil of separation to be torn in two, so that we might enter the most holy place: the presence of the Father. And we do not enter as enemies or as representatives of some neutral celestial kingdom. We enter as sons, as people who can rightfully bear the name of Theophilus: those who love God. This is the Spirit within us, killing the anti-spirit, causing us to love him according to the way He established. This is by keeping his commandments so that we might enter boldly into his presence. This is not the boldness of arrogance, or of one owed something. It is the boldness of one who is loved and loves.

This is the great movement of God and what the doctrine of the Trinity reveals. He is the goal, the avenue, and the impeller. There is no empty space, no area left open. In every way it is God who works and who purposes, so where is our boasting? There is none! Where is the possibility of failure? There is none! There is nothing left to do but be filled with true love and true joy, appreciating what each person has done for us and fully immerse ourselves in that truth. We must align our theological focus along the path of God, approaching him on his terms. At a very basic level this is illustrated in prayer. We pray to the Father, as Jesus taught us. It is in the name of the Son that we can so boldly speak to the Father. And it is Spirit himself who teaches us to pray. Every aspect is covered: the goal, the means, and the will—all of it by God.

WHAT THE TRINITY TEACHES INDIVIDUALS

There is one overarching way that our understanding of the Trinity should inform our individual lives. It is that the members of the Trinity act in the love of God. There is never a moment when one member does not love the others, and it is this love we have been given. It is the thing Christ prayed for on behalf of his disciples. This love causes God to act as one for the plan of God, and the different persons to take on individual roles for this plan. The roles they take correspond to each person's nature and place in the Trinity.

Consider the Son. There was never a point when the Father or the Spirit would become incarnate because the Son, as the Logos, is the expression of God. Since he is this perfect expression of God, it only makes sense that he should enter into the world to reveal the Father. He was not created for this purpose or forced into this role, but the role and the purpose was created by the Father for him. Consider John 17:4 where Jesus says, "I have finished the work which You have given Me to do." Though faced with the humility of being a man, of being obedient, of being despised by those who should have loved him, of being rejected, and in spite of murder he met the task.

We are told in Hebrews 12:2 that, "For the joy set before Him [Jesus] endured the cross, despising the shame, and has sat down at the right hand of the throne of God." There are two things to notice in this verse from Hebrews. The first is that Jesus acted because of the *joy* set before him. Surprisingly it was not the fame or the glory but the joy that was motivating him. What exactly was this joy? The answer is in the second point I want to make, and it is that the joy was not only to be found at the end of the affair. While the end of it all was to sit down at the right hand of God, this was not all of the joy, for Jesus would merely be returning to the place he had come from. For consider his words in John 17:5 where he says, "And now, O Father, glorify Me together with Yourself, with the glory which I had with You before the world was." Are we to conclude that Jesus possessed no authority before his incarnation, death, resurrection, and ascension? Certainly not! For if he possessed a shared glory with the Father then this must certainly be understood to have been a shared authority with God. So the joy set before Christ was not merely a return to glory, for if one goes on a quest the aim is not merely to return home. If that was the case, then one would achieve the goal by never leaving home. There is some purpose to a quest that can only be fulfilled by leaving. So the joy set before Jesus must have been something else. Of course, he has worked to save his people, and this cannot be ignored, but there is a deeper purpose and this is the fulfillment of the Father's will. This includes everything before he sat down at the right hand of the Father, for even in the shame Christ experienced there was a joy which made the shame of no lasting consequence. There was that same joy throughout the entirety of the incarnation. It was a joy that led up to and continues in Christ's current position. This tells us that the motivating factor for Jesus was the glorification of God by being obedient to the Father.

It is a sign of human sin that for us obedience usually entails some kind of force or coercion. We don't *want* to obey—ever. When you were a child you didn't want to clean your room. As a teenager you didn't really want to do *anything* your parents told you to do. As an adult, do you ever really want to pay your taxes? Do you *want* to drive the speed limit? And what if your parents now tell you that you *must* do or not do something? Perhaps you honor their opinion, but is your natural reaction joyful obedience? Or would you think something like *I'm an adult now, you can't tell me what to do*? But this is not at all the attitude of God the Son. It is not as though God the Father is forcing him to do anything. That would be like reading John 3:16 as saying, "For God so love the world that He forced his only begotten Son into the world..." But this isn't the case. There was never any forcing, never any coercion, because there never is any tension between the Father and Son because they share the same Spirit. The Father gives to the Son the glory of being Messiah because it gives the Father joy to do so. The Son in turn took on flesh, suffered, died, rose again, and is seated at the Father's right hand because it is a joy for him to obey the Father and go through with his plan.

Obedience for Jesus, though, was not just in agreeing to the overall plan of creating and redeeming the world. What Jesus agreed to was the role the Father had created for him: a role of a man, and being found as a man he humbled himself to obey God. This meant more than just agreeing not to lie or murder, covet, or fornicate. Jesus also had to actively obey as a man. He willing did all that was required of him as a man, even to the point of making sure his mother was taken care of after he died.[3] Obeying God meant going through the basic realities of life—things we take for granted because they are all we have ever known. It meant learning a trade from Joseph. It meant going to get water for his family, perhaps changing the diapers for his brothers and sisters. It meant keeping all the festivals laid out in the law. As a child he had to respect older men who were not worthy of respect. He lived with his people under the rule of lawless pagans! He paid the temple tax when it was his own house!

To be obedient as a man may not seem that interesting to us, but that is only because we do not remember what it was like to exist before becoming a man or a woman. But Jesus remembered what it was like before taking on the human nature. What else could it mean when he said, "Glorify Me together with Yourself, with the glory which I had with You before the world was," unless Jesus remembered what it was like to have had that glory before? So if there ever was a person on earth who could claim to be uncomfortable in his body it was Jesus because he could remember a time before his body—and that existence was glory itself. Yet he set it aside and

3. John 19:25–27.

took upon himself the human nature, and not just any nature. He became a man, a male. He took up certain responsibilities which, if he was truly to obey the Father, he needed to do. It would have been easy enough for him to snap his fingers and transform himself into anything he wanted: a Roman, a woman, an eagle, a rock. He could have done any of these things, but instead he willingly and joyfully accepted the role the Father gave him as a first century man in Judea. It was not just a physical form. It was a life and a series of expectations he accepted—not the expectations of men, but the expectations laid out in the Father's creative and revealed will. He became a man because that is what the Father decided for him.

There is something so incredibly valuable and joyful in knowing the Father that Jesus was willing to obey—not just in coming as a man, but by obeying as a man. It should give us insight into what Jesus is actually calling his disciples to when he said, "If you love Me, keep My commandments."[4] The Lord was not saying something out of the blue. He was not demanding this because he is an unbearable tyrant. No, it was experiential knowledge of what it means to love. He simply commands his disciples to do the same thing he did! But notice the order: if you love *then* obey. The one flows from the other, but you cannot have the one without the other. What this teaches us is that if we want to love the Son and the Father, then we will obey what God has commanded. It means despising those things which do not measure up to the joy of loving God; that is, despising those things which are the antithesis to his commands.

Notice that I do not say the joy of being loved by God. Too often the Christian focus is on that half, on the part of being loved by God, and do not be mistaken. It is an important half of the equation. But it is only half. The other half is *getting* to love God by obeying him. It is a joyous thing for the Son to obey his Father by fulfilling the role created for him. In the same way we should find joy in obeying the Father by fulfilling the roles he has created for us. I do not mean this in a sort of minor messianic way. I am afraid popular fiction, especially fantasy, has taught people that there is an utterly unique thing that each person must do in the world, something they and only they can do. This plays to human vanity, but it is not the role I am talking about.

Not everyone is given the role of a king, president, governor, apostle, prophet, or teacher, but everyone has been given a role. This role might be that of a man or a woman, a single person or in a marriage, it might be the

---

4. John 14:15.

role of an elder or of a younger, a rich person or poor person, slave or free, child or adult. Into each of these roles God has poured certain rights and responsibilities, none of which are to be abused, and all of which are to be enjoyed. They are not empty shells or offices to be filled by just anyone. Rather God has bound them to and into our very lives, creating us male or female, touching our very souls by being married or single, slave or free. They are not jobs we clock in and out of for eight hours of work. They are rightfully called *life*, and the beauty of it is that each man is not every man, and each woman not every woman. There is a uniqueness of person and circumstance that creates something wonderful, even though the commands given by God are general. For God does not give every husband a unique set of commands. He says to all husbands of all time, "Love your wives." But the application of this across time, cultures, and individuals results in such diverse beauty as is found in a forest, where all the trees, though similar, possess unique traits that mark them from one another, and where every flower has its own radiance though all the same kind of flower. These silent creatures understand what so many do not understand, and it is that we are to love the type of thing God has made us, and to do what it is he has commanded us to do as man and woman, flower or tree. It is like a painter who at the foundation of everything is using the same base colors, but with which he makes a masterpiece. It is like the Trinity: each person beautifully being God and yet doing so as the Father, the Son, and the Spirit respectively.

What God's Trinitarian nature teaches us is that it is not a shameful thing to obey the Father. Far from it! It is a good thing when, being found in the form of a man or woman, we follow those commands given to men and women, even as Jesus followed the commands given for Jewish men. But it is not obedience to the letter of the law, but to the Spirit of the law, for the Spirit calls us to love God. The difference may seem subtle, but what it boils down to is motivation. We obey God's law because we want to, because it is our Father's law and our Savior's law.

This is something the world cannot and will not understand. The world will not understand it because it has the wrong spirit. The world says men are toxic and that the best thing for you men to do is spend your days playing video games—though of course, the world will mock you for doing this. The world says to women that to be a woman of value you need to be more like men. The world creates categories for men and women, and while in one breath the world says there is no difference, in the other the world says if you do not match its categories exactly then maybe you are really the other gender. Or in economic matters the world tells the poor they deserve the wealth of the wealthy, while at the same time the spirit of the world pushes people to give up everything good to earn a little more money. All the while, no matter what it is, the world says you should do everything you can to be happy while giving you nothing of real happiness.

There is no joy in what the world offers. You will never truly be happy with your body: you could always be stronger, thinner, bigger, younger, or older. The fact is that in one area or another you might feel you don't quite live up to what it means to be a man or a woman. The truth is you may work harder than anyone else you know and yet not be wealthier than them. These are the brute realities we face. It's the reality that Jesus faced. There was nothing physically mighty about him. By some standards of the world he never lived up to fully being a man because he never fathered children. He worked exceedingly hard, but had no home to call his own. None of these things mattered because he was not seeking to please the world, or even himself. He found joy in pleasing the Father.

This is where joy is found. No matter what you are born as or born with, no matter how much you make or don't make, no matter the circumstance you find yourself in, your focus, as one filled with the Spirit, is to determine by how best to obey God. Throw your entire life into it. Because it is the *life* that God has given you: not just your sex, not just your career, not just your marital status, not just your ethnicity, or your economic status. It is all of these and more, because life is all of these and more.

It was said of Jesus that for the joy set before him he endured the cross. I would dare add to this that, for the joy set before him, Jesus endured human life. He endured all the things I listed before: childhood and being obedient and honoring to Mary and Joseph. He learned a trade and did work. He obeyed the Torah. And it is not just that he endured it, but within it He found joy because he was obeying his Father. He could say, "Father, I have finished the work You gave to Me." Can the same be said of us? Do we endure manhood and womanhood with joy because God assigned us male or female—and yes, he does assign such things! Are assignments fun? Not necessarily, but we should find joy in it because it is from our Father in heaven. We must endure being black or white or yellow or red or polka dot. Actually, we must do more than endure; we must find joy in it because our Heavenly Father painted us this color. We must not only endure poverty, but find joy in it because God gave us poverty. We must not only endure wealth but find proper joy in it because God has made us wealthy.

This is what the Trinity teaches us as individuals. The individual persons of God are motivated in their very being by love for God. Each one loves God by taking on particular roles. The Son is particularly our model because he became a human. He found joy in what God assigned him. He finished the work in its entirety, loving God by obeying the Father in all of life. When Yahweh commands us to love the LORD our God with all our heart, soul, mind, and strength he is only telling us to do what he himself does in his individual persons.

WHAT THE TRINITY TEACHES THE CHURCH

Closely linked to individual application is corporate application. God is three in one so that the one is just as important as the three, and the three just as important as the one. Put another way, the three persons of God exist as three distinct persons, but their oneness in God is so perfect that there can be no tension or disunite among them. There is absolute unity within absolute diversity, and both are defined by love.

The mutual love among the members of God is an equal love, but it does not have the same flavor. I mean a son's love for his father is different than the love a father has for his son. They are different in their polarity though they share the same magnet and they complement one another. So too in the Trinity the Son's love, though equally perfect and equally potent as the Father's, manifests itself different in that the Son is obedient to the Father and not vice versa. The Father, on the other hand, loves the Son by giving him prominence in all things, glorifying him by using him. In the same way a husband's love is not the same as his wife's love for him, though both claim to share the same marital love. It should be obvious, then, whether speaking of God or human relationships, love is not a monolithic thing. There are differences, and this is what makes love complete and marvelous.

The same is true within the churches. There are many, many differences among the members of the church. There are differences in economic status, in skin color, in abilities, in sex, in background, and all sorts of other things, and these differences are important. The differences in roles, abilities, and obedience give different tones, shapes, and shades to the picture God is painting. Therefore no one should despise any other for his role and gifting. The Spirit does not despise the Son for his prominent role nor does the Son despise the Spirit for his less prominent role. Each is well pleased to love and serve the Father in his respective role, and so too each of us should find great joy in the particular role we have been given.

It can be difficult to find joy in one's role if you don't actually know what your role is in the church. Preachers, teachers, and musicians seem to have it all figured out, but what about those who feel no inclination to speak in front of everyone, or to teach, or who cannot even clap in rhythm with an upbeat song? This is an important question, and it can be answered. It is answered first by those general commands given to those in your particular situation. Women are given commands by God that are only for them, and the same is true for men. Older people are given instructions that younger people cannot yet carry out (see Titus 2). A slave is not at liberty to travel great distances to preach. A wealthy man has been given disposable income to serve God. Each of these things must be kept in mind when considering how any individual member of the church is to function. It is not all about Sunday morning. Church life is not all about singing or teaching or listening. To take this approach to the church would be like thinking the most important part of all of redemption was the cross.

Now that almost sounds heretical, doesn't it? But think about it. If the cross was the single most important work of God, then what are we to say about creation? What are we to say about the giving of the scriptures? What of regeneration and sanctification? What shall we say of the Father putting all the Son's enemies under his feet? What are we to say of the Son giving the kingdom to the Father? None of these things can be said to be less important than the cross, even if they appear less prominent. They each serve a function that is important and cannot be done away with if God's plan is to be completed. So too the different members of the church who serve at different times and in different ways are no less important to the overall purpose of the church to display the wisdom of God, even if they are less prominent.

Now while this talk of the diversity within the church is important, there is a second way the Trinity informs our relations with one another, and that is in unity. Perhaps the best place for a description of what this unity is can be found in John 17:20–16. There Jesus prays for those of us who would believe in him because of the witness of the Apostles. This is such an amazing thing! In the night that he was betrayed Jesus prayed for us! He speaks to the Father concerning us, and asks something very special and very important. He asks that, "they all may be one, as You, Father, are in Me, and I in You; that they may also be one in Us…that they may be as one just as We are one." Consider what Jesus is asking for. He has already expressed that he is not the Father in that he does a work the Father assigned to him. Yet they are one. Certainly they are one being, one substance, but is Jesus asking this for his disciples?

This is a tricky question. We do not become God, nor do we become little gods, as some heresies might suggest. Nevertheless Jesus expresses an intimacy within God that is being shared with us. He says just as He is in the Father and the Father in him, so too he wants the disciples to share this kind of unity. To this He links the idea of love by saying, "And I have declared to them Your name, and will declare it, that the love with which You have loved Me may be in them, and I in them." This unity, this thing that makes the Father in the Son and the Son in the Father, is also the love they share. If you will remember from a previous chapter, I argued that the love of God is the Holy Spirit. It is he who causes the Father to be in the Son and the Son in the Father. It is the Spirit who is the very love of God which is shared by the Father and Son and which is extended to the disciples. As Peter says, we are partakers of the divine nature.[5] We are partakers of this unifying spirit.

Sometimes we Christians get a bit vague when it comes to actually explaining what it means to be unified in the Spirit. Sometimes we think it is primarily a feeling, but it's more than a feeling. As we just finished talking about a few minutes ago, the love Jesus has for the Father expresses itself in obedience. The Father's love is expressed in the glorification of the Son. While the expressions differ, the love is what unites God, just as surely as his own being unites him. This is the same thing which is to unify the church with its diversity, for there are numerous roles and gifts, but there is just one love. There are leaders and followers, but one Spirit. While there are men and women in the church, the same God is over and in them. There are different ethnicities and different skin colors, but they are painted by the same Artist. There are different roles but the same focus: to love and obey God.

This is something our culture struggles with. There are loud voices clamoring that diversity is essential, and that this diversity is to somehow produce unity. But, of course, diversity itself can never produce unity. Diversity is like an explosion, each element going its own way based on its

5. 2 Pet. 1:3–4

own trajectory. On the other side of the spectrum are those who refuse to acknowledge diversity, who argue that people must be the same in the church: the same skin color, the same economic status, or the same role. Everyone must be the same. What our culture and our world cannot do is bring these things into proper and perfect harmony. No political party, no philosophy, and no other religion can give an answer. Only Christianity, only the Trinitarian God can say to people, be one as we are one, because only in the Trinitarian God are both diversity and unity held perfectly. Only God himself is the perfect example of what it means for these things to be perfectly true. And Jesus asks that we might be one as he and the Father are one.

What an amazing request! This oneness does not abolish individuality. It does not abolish the unique gifts we have been given. It does not make meaningless the differences between men and women, old and young, or the differences between people with different skin colors. The unity Jesus speaks of does not destroy these differences; it makes them meaningful and beautiful. The different responsibilities, the different roles, and the different backgrounds of individual disciples create a mosaic of obedience if we are all striving toward the common goal of loving God with our heart, soul, mind, and strength. We should glory in each person's loving obedience, just as the Son is glorified in glorifying the Father.

This love unites us; this Spirit animates us, and calls us to live a certain way toward one another. For this reason Paul says, "Let no corrupt word proceed out of your mouth, but what is good for necessary edification, that it may impart grace to the hearers. And do not grieve the Holy Spirit of God, by whom you were sealed for the day of redemption. Let all bitterness, wrath, anger, clamor, evil speaking be put way from you, with all malice. And be kind to one another, tenderhearted, forgiving one another, even as God in Christ has forgiven you."[6] Those things that grieve the Holy Spirit of God are exactly those things which make it impossible to fellowship. You cannot stand to be in the presence of someone if you are keeping bitterness in your heart against them. You will not long fellowship if you are full of wrath, or are angry, or are clamorous toward those in church. They will not long fellowship with you if malice fills your soul. But if you truly want to love God and enjoy the Spirit, then you will be kind. You will choose to be tenderhearted. You will be forgiving instead of brooding. You will not begrudge another person his gift, or station. You will rejoice in that each of

6. Eph 4:29–31.

us has a different role, and be glad when each of us is glorifying God by act-ing in obedience. But you will only do this if you share in the unity which God gives: the Spirit of God.

Our culture needs the unifying Spirit. Our churches need it. Right now there are those professing to be Christians who say if you have black skin you should not fellowship in churches that are composed of mixed ethnicities or are predominantly white.[7] Think about that! Is not Christ's body composed of men and women from all tribes and nations? Did not the same Spirit descend on the Jews and then the Gentiles alike? Is there not one God who commands us to love our neighbors? What business do these people have destroying the church of the living God? Such people share the same spirit as those who would destroy the bodies of young men and women who have not learned to love what God has made them. Such people share the same spirit as those who would sacrifice babies to the god of sex and convenience. This is not the Holy Spirit. This is not the Spirit which unites us in Christ, and makes us partakers of the divine nature. It is the spirit of the devil himself.

The Spirit of God which unites the people of God is that Spirit which breaks down the walls between us and makes our differences meaningful. Yes, meaningful. God does not make us color-blind. He makes us appreci-ate the colors that make up his beautiful church. Only when we realize that in our diversity and unity we reflect God himself will we be able to love one another boldly, in the way Paul described: in long-suffering, in kindness, without envy, without parading, without being puffed up, without being rude, without seeking our own, without being provoked, but rejoicing in truth, bearing all things, and hoping all things.[8] Only by having the right perspective of God, can we have a right perspective of ourselves. Only when this happens, and we work toward the common goal of loving God in obedience, will racial divides be broken down, and ethnic differences enjoyed. Only then will the differences between men and women be joyous differences. Only then will the variety of gifts be appreciated by all. Only then will real vitality and meaning be experienced by the church. Only in this way can complex diversity have absolute unity. Only, that is, if we know the wonderful doctrine of the Trinity.

7. Henny, "Have You Left Yet?" https://thewitnessbcc.com/why-havent-you-left-yet/.

8. 1 Cor 13:4–7.

10

Chopping Trees and Eating Turnips

Trees have no dogmas. Turnips are singularly broad-minded.

—G.K. CHESTERTON[1]

IT IS ONE THING to act as a tree or a turnip and keep our religion internal and merely a religion, but it is another thing entirely to be a human. To be human is to take those things held most dear, most sacred, and most true and apply them to real life. For if the things which are most dear, most sacred, and most true are not in fact real then they are illusions and good for little more than escapism and entertainment. Anyone whose religion and doctrine can never be brought to bear on the real world is rightfully chastised by those who say he must be more tolerant. On the other hand, anyone whose religion and doctrine can and often is brought to bear on the realities of the world cannot be tolerant; he must either be proven wrong or agreed with. Such a one not only guards truth in his heart, but unabashedly declares that this truth applies to all men in all situations and in all fields.

Evangelicalism has been criticized for withdrawal from serious study and scholarship, for having no philosophical input that can compete with secular authorities on matters such as history, physics, economics, or government.[2] This is due to a variety of things, but at its heart there seems to be some sort of disconnect between theology and philosophy, between

1. Chesterton, *Heretics*, 197.
2. Noll, *Scandal of the Evangelical Mind*, 10–23.

faith and life, and between the church and state. These things are separate from one another; perhaps it is because Evangelicals feel no one will listen, or perhaps these things are seen as irrelevant. Generally speaking, the world is perceived as marching inevitably toward hell; things are getting progressively worse, and some day all Christians will be beamed away. What is interesting about this is that so many Evangelicals argue against the kind of things that are supposed to usher in the final doom of the world: the deterioration of morality, the rise of a single currency, and associated things. This schizophrenic stance illustrates that deep down we want to speak Christianity into the world. Deep down we want the work of God to be seen in the world, and the truth of God to inform the world.

The world desperately needs truth. It desperately needs an option not only for religious matters, but for all of life: for art, for literature, for philosophy, for justice, and government. While I do not claim to offer anything like what is needed, this chapter attempts to show how the doctrine of the Trinity does indeed speak to the wider world: specifically, in the areas of worldview, government, and justice. I do not pretend that these suggestions are fully fleshed out, or that they will gain any attention or traction in the wider world. Nevertheless I offer them as a starting point for further conversation and action. Christians are not trees and they are not turnips for we have convictions and while we may be labeled as bigots and fools, Chesterton was correct when he said, "In real life the people who are the most bigoted are the people who have no convictions at all."[3] Those without convictions hold to them fervently and try to make everyone see life that way, even if this is inconsistency. Such people are fools, but no more foolish than those who claim to have life-encompassing truth but never seek to apply it to all of life. Let us not be fools, but apply the truth of God's nature to all areas of life so that we might offer truth and hope to those around us by standing upon the Solid Rock of our God.

WORLDVIEW

The first area of consideration is worldview. Everyone has a worldview, even if they have forgotten it. This is probably the situation for most people, Christians included, but as Christians we should not be satisfied with this. Our worldview is what sets us apart from the world—at least it is supposed to. And above all we should have a worldview, and be able to provide a

3. Chesterton, *Heretics,* 201.

reason for it, because it is our hope. So what, exactly, is a worldview? And what does this have to do with the Trinity?

There are several possible definitions for *worldview* depending on who you consult.[4] Some, such as James Sire, take a more philosophical approach, defining a worldview as "a commitment, a fundamental orientation of the heart, that can be expressed as a story or in a set of presuppositions ... that we hold ... about the basic constitution of reality, and that provides the foundation on which we live and move and have our being."[5] He then offers eight basic questions which worldviews answer:

1. What is prime reality—the really real?

2. What is the nature of external reality, that is, the world around us?

3. What is a human being?

4. What happens to a person at death?

5. Why is it possible to know anything at all?

6. How do we know what is right and wrong?

7. What is the meaning of human history?

8. What personal, life-orienting core commitments are consistent with this worldview?[6]

This definition has a particularly philosophical flavor, as Sire readily admits. A more anthropological example is found in Paul Hiebert's work *Transforming Worldviews*, where the following definition is given. Worldview is "the foundational cognitive, affective, and evaluative assumptions and frameworks a group of peoples makes about the nature of reality which they use to order their lives."[7] You can see the subtle shift from what is philosophically individualistic to a more community or group-minded perspective.

David Naugle offers another definition of worldview which he bases on the biblical concept of the *heart*. After providing the scriptural evidence for the importance of the *heart*, Naugle says, "Consequently, human existence proceeds 'kardioptically' on the basis of a vision of the heart, for

4. See Sire, *Naming the Elephant*, for a discussion of the concept of *worldview* and Naugle, *Worldview*, for a more in-depth discussion.

5. Sire, *Universe Next Door*, 20.

6. Sire, *Universe Next Door*, 22–23

7. Hiebert, *Transforming Worldviews*, 25–26.

according to its specific disposition, it grinds its own lenses through which it sees the world. According to the Bible, therefore, I propose that the heart and its content as the center of human consciousness creates and constitutes what we commonly refer to as a *Weltanschauung* [worldview]."[8] This definition should strike a chord with something, or rather someone, who has already been discussed. The Spirit is himself the gift given to replace a *heart* of stone. In other words, the vision of the heart is transformed by the work of the Spirit in our lives. This results in a shift not only of attitude, (as displayed in the fruit of the Spirit) but a shift of perspective, of assumptions, of community, and of what we understand reality to be. The Spirit informs us and impels us to actions and purpose so that he not only provides the worldview, but can rightfully be said to be the worldview.

Consider what the Spirit does. He presses upon our hearts the knowledge and love of God. This is the knowledge that Yahweh is the only true God and therefore the only source of reality: the really real. The Spirit informs us by means of his word what the universe is and what its purpose is. This is not an exhaustive, mechanical understanding of how the world works, but why it exists. At the same time it does not mean we must forever use the simplistic statement of "God caused it" without ever explaining how God might do it. The universe around us exists, and the Spirit prompts a love of God and an admiration for what he has done. Love for the maker will stimulate and guide what is known as scientific inquiry, but from a biblical perspective it would be better called philosophy, that is, the pursuit of wisdom. When God is the definer of truth and the mechanisms of the world, then everything we consider science is touched by theology.

There is, of course, the danger which has been experienced throughout Christendom, which is the magisterializing of knowledge. Galileo is the oft cited example of this, for his observations were perceived as conflicting with biblical revelation. The authorities of that time failed to appreciate how God expresses truth and the different means by which he has done this. Scholars, such as John Walton argue that the Bible tells us that God did indeed create and does indeed sustain all things, but that it does not tell us how this is done. Walton is adamant that Christians must read the Bible as God intended and this means understanding what the original authors intended. The scriptures do record events, but primarily it is God telling us how we are to understand the events as opposed to explaining the mechanisms which were used to cause the events. While one may not agree with

8. Naugle, *Worldview*, 270.

Walton, what he rightly draws our attention to is that there are two types of revelation: special and general. Man can know things about the universe either because God specifically reveals them or because he has created man to be able to know things. It is the church's job to understand clearly what things are revealed in each category.

That we can know anything at all stems from Christ's nature as the Logos of God. While it is true that God created people to be able to know things, it is also true that unless reality communicates to us in ways we understand (or can eventually understand) we will never know reality. We never know a closed door is there unless we see it or walk into it. But doors are dependant reality in that they depend on the really real to exist. They depend on God to exist. Something that depends on something else for existence also depends on that same thing for revelation. It is not merely that God creates the universe and everything inside of it, but he communicates it to the minds of his conscious creatures. It is the inverse of what we would expect because creation reveals certain things about God, but it only does so because God communicates himself in his Logos. Communication exists of the perfect (God communicated through the Logos) and serves as the basis for communication and understanding of the imperfect (knowledge of the universe). In this way God's Triune nature is foundational to the knowledge aspect of the Christian worldview. We can know because God has purposefully communicated himself.

Once this cornerstone of the Trinitarian Worldview is laid, then everything else falls into place. Those things concerning man, his place in universe, his relationship to God, his fate, and purpose come into focus because God not only reveals himself, but his Spirit reveals his temperament and plan. In fact, it is this plan (as discussed in chapter 4) that provides the outline of history. Without it there is no purpose and there can be no theology, no anthropology, no historiography, no philosophy, nothing. But because of God's revelation of himself and his plan each of these categories can be addressed. Simply consider the questions posed by Sire. The answers to these rely upon the Trinity for their clearest expression. God's revealed plan is not merely a story; it is a myth, but in the proper sense. It is a living story, a descriptor of who we are and where we come from and where we are going. And at its heart the story is that of a kingdom and Jesus Christ is the King. Every thought, every desire, every world system, and every other kingdom and government is being subjected to him.

GOVERNMENT

It may seem a strange shift to move from worldview to government, but at the present time there is a need in the United States, and perhaps in the wider world, for a positive argument for what government should be based upon the Trinitarian worldview. The presentation here is not, as one might expect, primarily reliant on Christ's position as the King of kings and Lord of lords, though certainly every nation is commanded to obey the rule of Christ. The Judge of the world will indeed judge those rulers and principalities on whether their work was in accordance with Romans 13:4, but there is a deeper question, one concerning the nature of government itself. A person could conclude that because Jesus is King he has appointed little kings in the world to act as his representatives. This may have been true for a large period of human history in many nations, but it does not accurately represent all of the data. There are, or have been, cultures without kings, such as the United States. This indicates that either such government types are sinful, or else the reality is that God institutes *government* and not merely kings.

This begs the question: what would a good government look like? Before this question can be answered it must be ascertained whether government is necessary primarily because men are sinners or if the concept of government possesses an eternal, indeed, a divine quality.

There are some who view government as a necessary evil, and others who find it to be an unnecessary evil. There are still others who find government to be a good thing, and that it can and should do as much as possible to do positive good for its citizens. The current situation in the world is bringing this difference into sharp relief because there are some who believe governments should implement very strict laws to curb the spreading of COVID-19, while there are others who think lockdowns and mask or vaccine mandates are overstepping proper bounds. Then there is the issue of economic recovery and how much money should be spent to help those who are not working. It is interesting that there is not a united perspective offered by Christians in the matter of government, and there never has been. This because there is not a common theology of government. The particular traditions of which I have been a part (church and political) would argue that government is a necessary evil. But when changing the question from one of political philosophy to political theology it becomes evident that government is not only necessary but also good. It is inherent in the universe, even in God himself.

What do I mean by this? I mean that within God there is government, and that this government is the reality we are to reflect in humanity since we are made in the image of God. God does indeed govern himself. This is evident in the fact that he does what he pleases. No human ever really does what he pleases, not perfectly. But God does, and this is clear in the plan of creation, in the keeping of the promise symbolized by the rainbow, and by the maintenance of the covenants that include blessing and curses. It is evident in the Son becoming obedient to the point of death, and in the Spirit working in the lives of God's people. Would we say that the Son and Spirit *must* be governed because if they were not then the Son would rob the Father of divinity? Certainly not! But what we can say is that that Son and Spirit submit to the will of the Father and this in no way changes their equality in God. As the perfect Being and ultimate reality God serves as a model for the human system. For like God we find in creation and in humanity the fundamental nature of the Trinity: the absolute expressions of unity and diversity.[9] The unity of God is bound up in the glorification of God and each member of the Trinity acts to carry out this will of God.

This is the first principle of God's governance: within himself there is absolute unity and diversity. Never does this change; never does one dilute the other. This principle is found throughout creation, and it is an important element of the Trinitarian worldview.[10] It also informs human governments; for from the most totalitarian dictatorship to the most liberal democracy, what defines them is unity and diversity. This relationship is not merely in the governed verses the governors, but is to be present in the very nature of government itself. In governing himself each person of God has taken on particular roles, each of which is absolutely essential to God for they are the embodiment of each person's nature. The Father is the Originator, the Son the Expresser, and the Spirit the Temperament. These three work in harmony to live as God.

The Father is the Originator, the source of the governance and its will. The Son and the Spirit carry this will out, giving in freely to the Father's will. In human government this same relationship exists. There is always a will at work; of course God's Providential will is always at work, but I mean the will tied to the government itself. This might be a dictator who gives out laws according to what he desires. It might be that of the people as a whole, such as is claimed at in the preamble of the United States Constitution,

9. Bavink, *Reformed Dogmatics*, 234.

10. Rogusa, "Trinity at the Center of Thought and Life," 154–55.

but most clearly expressed in direct democracies such as those found in ancient Athens. Or there may be a sort of generational will that is created by one generation and passed on to another in the form of constitutional law. Whichever the case, we find the will at work attempting to motivate the governed. A dictator may lavish gifts on his people, do things to fill their life with the fear of death, or else try to deify themselves so the people will not only obey but worship. In democracies the will of the government is usually enforced through debate, conviction, or bribery. Constitutional or generational will requires education to maintain that will. But within God there is no such wrangling, fear, or bribery. The Son and Spirit work in the Father's plan for the sake of love and in this way possess a singular spirit or will.

This singular will of God is expressed and carried out by the active principle of God: the Logos. The Logos expresses the Father and his will, and it is the Logos by whom all things are created. The Son is also the one to rule all the nations and who will judge the living and the dead. Humans emulate this by expressing the will of the ruler through proclamations or codification of laws. Humans also enforce these proclamations or laws and this is through coercion or force. There is not a government on earth that makes oral or written laws and which does not also use taxation, policing, or the military to carry out that will. Whether the people are in harmony with the will of the ruler or not will determine what kind of force is needed.

This is what is so perfect and unique about God. The disharmony that humans experience between different persons is absent in God because of the Holy Spirit. He binds Father and Son together in harmonious love so that one directs and the other obeys without friction. In the same way any lasting government of men must have a temperament or spirit which unites the rulers and the ruled. Peace cannot be maintained within a government or action taken on the part of the people for the government unless there is a common spirit. A spirit of fear may do this, but usually in a totalitarian state the individual's greatest effort is given in times of greatest need. The glory of the Soviet Union was the Second World War because during that time the Soviet people's unifying spirit was not Communism, but defense and survival. During the 1960s a great disunity of spirit pervaded the United States, dissolving peace. At the same time there was a great national effort, a unification of spirit in one area that resulted in men walking on the moon. But, as the American Civil War and the current spirit of America demonstrates, a disunity of spirit results in friction, division, and an inability to act.

These four principles (unity/diversity, will, expression/action, and spirit) are present in all forms of government and this is because humans bear the image of God. This is not only true individually, but communally. What will be quite clear even in this brief discussion is that any imbalance and overemphasis in one area or another will result in instability in the government and the purpose of the government. What is also clear from history is that governments do fall and it is always a result of sin. It is because of this that the revelation of God is so important. It both condemns and instructs. Condemnation comes because within God we see such holy purity, unity, diversity, will, action, and spirit that an examination of ourselves reveals how unholy, foul, totalitarian, anarchical, aimless, overbearing, and distempered our own situation is. What the Trinitarian worldview offers is an accurate diagnosis of the problem and a perfect example to emulate.

Traditionally discussions about governments have focused on the issues of anarchy and tyranny, or on the forms of government: democracy, oligarchy, or monarchy. What the Trinitarian perspective offers are more foundational insights: unity and diversity, will, expression, active principle, and spirit. Governments must recognize the unity-diversity nature of humanity. Failure to do this will result in an inhuman government: whether it be a dictatorship or democracy. Governments must have a basis in some will: again it may be the will of one man or the will of the people, but there must and shall be some motivating will that guides the whole. This will must be expressed. It must be known by both government and governed, and in human experience this means written expression. There must, in addition to this expression, be action. This will be done through expenditure, building, regulating, or enforcing. Finally, there must be a unifying temperament. This can only come by individuals having an orientation of the mind and heart to do the will expressed. Not only this, but if it is to be sustained, the temperament must truly be one of love for both the government and the governed.

These are the basics of government, and what should be apparent is that the government described could be good or evil. The people as a whole might be evil, or the people might be foolish or afraid and the individual will guiding them might be evil. What this tells us is that the bare-bones mechanisms of Trinitarian government are insufficient to produce goodness in government. What we see in God is that he governs himself according to his own will, and he does so perfectly. That is because he is holy and true, eternal and absolutely sovereign. He has not only thought out the plan for creation-history, but has the will and ability to carry it out. Because of this, there is only one will that shall be successful in creation, and that is his. Any human government wanting to be good and lasting must therefore not only reflect God's form of government, but must also take up his Spirit and do what he has revealed. This should come as no surprise, for in the discussion of the Spirit of God and of individual application the necessity of obeying God's revealed will was seen to be central to loving God. So, in a word, the heart of Trinitarian government is *theonomy*: a society governed by the laws of God. This word dredges up terrible ideas for many people, even Christians, but at its heart and in its purest form, theonomy is summed up in this way: Love the LORD with all your heart, soul, mind, and strength; and love your neighbor as yourself.[11] It means worshipping God and doing justice to our fellow human beings.

JUSTICE

The Trinitarian ability to balance and harmonize unity and diversity means that it alone of all the systems is able to account for true justice. Today this is the topic of discussion in so many circles: people on the political left, right, people outside the church, and people within the church. There are riots in the streets: people burning cars and buildings in the name of justice. There are commentators on radio and on TV, bloggers and podcasters who decry the riots saying there is no justice in them. Everything is excused; everything is condemned. All of this because the world and the church have lost touch with what justice really is. To many people it has become a feeling and to others a utilitarian logic. Like the pagans of old, our modern culture knows that justice is good, but they do not know why justice is good. It is such a passionate feeling within them that an accusation of wrong-doing is enough to condemn, while being caught red-handed bears little consequence. No one is being taught justice, even in the churches. But justice should be taught. It should be thought about, and it should be derived from our understanding of who God is.

God wants his people to understand what justice is, and this should make Christians, more than anyone else, ready with a clear definition of it, and zeal for its execution. This is seen in Genesis 18 when Yahweh and two angels visit Abraham. After promising a child by Sarah, the LORD and

---

11. For an in-depth discussion of theonomy and its message of hope for current cultural affairs, see Boot, *Mission of God*.

the two men with him arise to look toward Sodom, and Abraham goes with. Then Yahweh says something interesting. He says, "Shall I hid from Abraham what I am doing, since Abraham shall surely become a great and mighty nation, and all the nations of the earth shall be blessed in him? For I have known him, in order that he may command his children and his household after him, that they may keep the way of the LORD, to do righteousness and justice, that the LORD may bring to Abraham what he has spoken to him." Notice the reason Yahweh says anything. It is so that Abraham may command his children and household to act righteously and to do justice. This is why Abraham got to see the destruction of the cities and why he got to try to bargain with God. It is why the Spirit includes it in his revelation. God links righteousness and justice, making it clear that these things are important not only for God but for his people. But God is not merely giving a hypothetical case. It is a most serious concept he is teaching, and it required a serious situation.

According to Yahweh, the outcry against Sodom and Gomorrah was great, and their sin very grave. This is especially illustrated in Genesis 19:11 when, even after being struck blind, the men wearied themselves trying to get at Lot's door. They did not go back to their own homes after darkness descended over their eyes. They kept trying to get their goal. So the sin of Sodom was very real and a very serious thing. But we must refrain, for our purposes, from getting sucked into the great debate about what exactly the sins of Sodom and Gomorrah were (though that seems clear enough from the text). The point we need to focus on is what Yahweh is doing, what his perspective is, and how it plays into the Trinitarian concept of justice.

Consider what occurs in Genesis 18:22–33. Abraham tries to bargain with God for the cities. But is it really a bargain? Is it not rather a question about what justice really is? For consider Abraham's question. Will God destroy the righteous and the wicked? That is the heart of the issue. Is it more important for God to destroy the wicked than to preserve the righteous? Abraham starts with asking whether 50 righteous people would be enough to stop the destruction. We are not told how many people lived in Sodom, but perhaps it was in the thousands. So even this initial number was likely not a large portion of the population. Nevertheless God says for that number he would spare the city. The number gets winnowed down to ten, and even then Yahweh promises to hold back wrath for their sake. When God's men enter the city and it becomes clear that there are not even ten righteous people, still God pulls Lot and his family out before raining fire and brimstone upon the cities. Yes, wrath comes, but there is also mercy.

In this lesson for Abraham and his descendants God shows the importance of separating innocent from guilty. More than this, the protection of the innocent is more important than the punishment of the guilty, or else God was a liar and would not have spared the city for ten righteous citizens. This is how God wants humans to operate. This is the kind of mindset he wants the descendants of Abraham to have and to bless the world with. But at the same time the vengeance of justice is not forgotten. Whether immediately, or at the ultimate end, Yahweh does bring justice. This is why Yahweh had to be the one to destroy these cities. It could not have been the band of raiders that attacked the city some time before. It had to be God acting in a clear and decisive way.

Another element God presents is providing witnesses against the guilty. God himself bears witness against the cities by saying the cry of their sin has ascended into heaven. He also bears witness by his two men entering the city, and by the conscience of Lot. While these three bore witness in different ways—God being all knowing, the Sodomites attempting to assault the men, and by Lot living among inhabitants—it only servers to strengthen the case against the cities. It is in accordance with the principles of a thing being confirmed by the mouths of two or three witnesses.

Once the witness has been given, and the grievous nature of the sin revealed, the punishment needed to be handed out. Had God failed to do this, then what kind of lesson would this have been for Abraham and his descendants? It would have illustrated that punishment was not an important part, and that it is sufficient to merely bring sin to light. But this does not fit with God's nature. Sin must be punished absolutely and completely because God is holy and preserves holiness. God demonstrates this in the destruction of the cities, for there was no weakness in his hand, only swift decisiveness. While the sin of Sodom and the surrounding cities might have been growing for decades or even centuries, when God finally rendered judgement the punishment came swiftly. This is another element of the justice of God: when judgment has been rendered it is carried out. There are no loose ends.

Now I said that this is Trinitarian justice, and so it is. The scripture is quite clear that Abraham spoke with Yahweh. What Jesus seems to indicate in John 8:56–58 is that it was he, the Son, whom Abraham saw when he says, "Your father Abraham rejoiced to see My day, and he saw it and was glad." Now it is tempting to say this is merely a reference to the promise of seed and the birth of Isaac, but this is not how the Jews took it. They reacted by saying, "You are not yet fifty years old, and have you seen Abraham?" Immediately after this Jesus says, "Before Abraham was, I Am," then the Jews tried to stone him. Now while Yahweh appears to Abraham in Genesis 12:7, we are not told in what form. It is really only in Genesis 18 that he is in the form of a man. Other biblical texts indicate no one has seen the Father at any time, so this must be the Son. This is further confirmed in Genesis 19:24 when it says, "Then the LORD rained brimstone and fire on Sodom and Gomorrah, from the LORD out of the heavens." Notice that Yahweh on earth rained destruction from Yahweh in the heavens. Yahweh on earth did not disappear and yet there was Yahweh in heaven. Here is one of the shadows of the Trinity present in the Old Testament and only fully realized after New Testament revelation.

What is most interesting is that Yahweh on earth judges the cities of Sodom and Gomorrah then calls down destruction from Yahweh in heaven. In other words, the Son seems to judge while the Father doles out the wrath. Where is the Spirit in this? He motivates the willingness to give mercy and the eventual bringing of justice to avenge holiness. He is the Spirit Yahweh is instilling in the heart of Abraham and his descendants: a Spirit of justice.

So we have this example in Genesis but does it answer the question of what justice actually is? While it is tempting to jump right to the idea of punishing the guilty and sparing the innocent, this is not the heart of the issue. The true core of justice rests in God. The destruction of Sodom and Gomorrah is, more than anything else, an illustration by God that he is the measure. Think of it. Abraham was not being injured by Sodom; in fact, he had just helped the Sodomites in battle only a little time before! No, God came because the outcry, the accusations against Sodom and the other cities offended him. Their sin was exceedingly great, and as has been previously discussed, sin is against God. All justice originates in him and because of him. Justice, then, is God giving to each according to the desires of his heart and the reality of his deeds. That God waited for the sins of Sodom and Gomorrah to grow indicates the reality of their conduct was important in justice. God did not destroy them just because their hearts were dark. He destroyed them because their lives were dark and against him. God has placed real meaning in the actions of men and this teaches us that we too should place real meaning in actions and not only in the heart.

Indeed, that God waited for actions instead of only judging the heart is to serve as a model for our own limitations. We cannot judge the heart apart from the actions, and so God teaches according to what we can learn.

God is the measure of justice in two ways. First he determines what is right and what is wrong. He does this through the type of revelation seen by all men and by special revelation. Chief among these is the value placed upon individual people, who are made in the image of God. All sin against men, all evil conduct, is directed at this. Everything from assault to murder, adultery, theft, and false witness is focused on the *imago dei* in humans. Attack an animal, kill it, steal from it and you will not have sinned. You may have demonstrated cruelty, but there is not a special value placed in animals as there is in man. Men and women alone of the creatures of the earth bear the image of God. There is such value placed on us by God that he assigned punishments for particular sins in his law, and this is the second way God is the measure of justice. By giving law and punishment God shows that there is value in the thing sinned against. Theft does not receive the same punishment as murder. By providing this differentiation he places value in our lives and in our property.

Human beings want offenses to be punished, but they want the punishment to fit the crime. In the heat of the moment the wronged party wants immediate and total justice: just ask any two year-old who has had her toy taken by another two year-old. That might be a funny image, but the only difference between her and the adult whose car was stolen is size of person and size of the object. The same heart is in them both: one that recognizes that *I* have been wronged. And who am I? Some traditions say that I am no one and that possessions (even one's own life) should be done away with because they bring only sorrow. The atheistic tradition may take pity on the one who suffered loss, but not because the tradition is consistent with itself. My empathy for someone suffering loss does not make sense if I am being atheistically consistent. In the Christian perspective, however, possessions do have meaning because human life has meaning. It is a meaning given by God in that he has made us in his image. It is this feature of the human being that makes us long for justice and judgment.

James 2:13 says that, "Mercy triumphs over judgement," but does this mean justice is abandoned? In other words, does mercy leave wrath unsatisfied? This may be the case for Allah, who, according to Sahih Bukhari, forgave a murderer based on whether he was closer to one city than to another.[12] Allah is able to forgive because he wants to, and never has to satisfy justice. The Trinitarian God, on the other hand, not only forgives but also satisfies justice. This is most clearly evident in Jesus Christ who bore the wrath of God so that those in him would not have to. He can only do this because not only is he perfect, but because God is the measure, he is the offended party in all situations. And he has such zeal for his holiness that justice will be done, even for those to whom he shows mercy.

There is no dangling thread. No sin, no wrong act, no offence, no hateful word, no rape, no murder, no theft, no wicked act that will go unpunished. This is the great confidence of Trinitarianism. God never winks at wickedness. God is never incapable of vengeance. He is never dismissive of the outcry of the oppressed because every wrong is against him, and his Spirit convicts the world of sin. And to those who cry out for mercy because of the blood of Christ he gives mercy. This is where ultimate satisfaction for justice rests: hope for those who comprehend their wickedness, satisfaction for those who have been wronged, and the terrible dread of certainty for those who are unrepentant.

To some, this idea of ultimate satisfaction is all well in good for spiritual matters, but they see no connection between it and the real world. The wrongs of centuries or of minutes seem unbearably immediate, and it is difficult to see that it is an eternal immediacy. It is difficult to see that every wrong is eternal in that it is against the eternal and infinite God. The wronged cry out for vengeance now! And there is a sense in which God does appoint governing authorities to punish evil doers now. Paul, in Romans 13:2–7, indicates that these authorities are intended to be a terror to those who do evil, wielding the sword killing those who deserve death. This speaks to the need for satisfaction, for wrongs to be avenged, not only eternally, but in the present. There is to be a spirit which binds people, a Holy Spirit which seeks justice. Truly this is an act of God that men should try to be just no matter the culture. Even unbelievers know in their heart of hearts that when the wicked go unpunished there is something wrong with the world. And so our culture has taken it upon itself to punish not only those proven to be wrong, but also merely accused of wrong—even if the accusation is proven false. This sits uneasily in the hearts of many, but for others zeal for some form of justice has eaten up all sense. There must be an alternative, and the Trinitarian worldview offers it.

12. Sahih Bukhari, "Merits of Sunnah," https://www.sahih-bukhari.com/Pages/Bukhari_4_56.php.

Yahweh's existence and revelation provides an unchanging law against which all actions should and will be judged. Atheism does not offer a source of moral judgement. The weak attempt by atheist Sam Harris to argue morality from science merely accepts several principles of biblical morality without adequately addressing why they are true.[13] The Trinitarian perspective grounds morality in the really real, in God's holiness. As such God is the one who must and will be avenged. No action is too slight or too grand, no human is too small or too big to fail. Wrath will come for every sin. This is a good thing, and governments exist to meet this need. They are to meet it upon fair and equal terms. By this I mean that the punishment fits the crime in so far as humans can do this.

At the same time the Trinitarian perspective offers a satisfactory mechanism of mercy. Those who are in Christ receive mercy because justice has already been satisfied. Even a persecutor of the church such as Paul found mercy because his persecution was already punished in Christ. This is the satisfactory mechanism of mercy even in a temporal setting. Those who truly repent can find mercy at the magistrate only if the price has been paid. Freeing prisoners or staying an execution does not satisfy justice unless someone actually has born wrath. Only if Christ is a part of the picture can this ever be done.

Of course, all of this hinges upon the Trinitarian God. It is theocratic in that sense, but it is nonetheless a viable system. What must be realized is that no matter what system a culture has it requires a common spirit in order for justice to be maintained. This is why pagan systems could recognize what was right and what was wrong, why they could speak of sin and focus on justice. There was a common spirit that found its basis in something immortal. Even atheists like Sam Harris recognize the need for a common spirit in that he tries to place morality into the hands of amoral science. If anyone does not buy into the system he places himself above the law. The more people who refuse to hold onto the system the less viable the justice system will be. In other words, if there is not a common spirit there cannot be common justice.

Inconsistency is the main cause of dissatisfaction in a judicial system. What few realize is that inconsistency comes from not knowing what the foundation for justice is. Today people want justice, but they do not know what it would mean for justice to truly be served. Christians, more than any other people, have the opportunity to offer clarity for justice, government

13. Harris, *Moral Landscape*, 15–19; 31–32; 42–46.

and worldview by nature of the Triune God. What I hope you have seen in this chapter is a glimpse of how our theology addresses these culturally important topics. Our society spends so much time and money on issues of government and justice. Every news outlet focuses on them. And every school, college, and university is concerned not only with these things, but in shaping the worldview of individual minds. Failure to address these things by the truth of our God is to fail to live in the Kingdom of God. For our God is not interested in pulling us out of the world. He has left us here to be salt and light. We are his leaven: such a small ingredient, but ballooning out and giving life to the entire loaf. He calls to us and through us to the world. He is not just giving certain laws and commands, but ever he calls one thing in particular: "Be perfect as I am perfect."

11

Divine Logos and Human Logos

> But I say that for every idle word men may speak, they will give account
> of it in the day of judgment.
>
> —MATTHEW 12:36

I HAD INTENDED THE previous chapter to be the last one before the conclusion, but there is an idea, an application of the doctrine we have been
discussing that I feel must be written down. It concerns Christ as the divine
Word of God and his relationship to our words. To be honest, I have tried
several different times to write out what exactly the idea is, but invariably it
became too complex, too much an attempt to deal with different interpre-
tive approaches to the Bible. Time after time I set it aside because it never
came out right, but time after time it would come back to my mind. So here,
in this chapter, I offer the most basic expression of this idea. Perhaps it is
foolish, and perhaps it is a misapplication of the doctrine, but if nothing
else it will show my conviction that our understanding of God's Trinitarian
nature is more than a religious truth. It has application to all sorts of things,
even to human communication.

In the same way that God's self-governance is reflected in human
government, God's communication is reflected in human communication. By using the term *reflected* I want to emphasize the point that all that
follows here is based on the idea that man is made in the image of God,
bearing qualities that show what he is like, and among these qualities is

communication. To a lesser extent animals communicate to one another, but they do not communicate with *words* and this is where the reflection takes place.

Within the Godhead there is someone communicating (the Father), someone who is the communication (the Logos), and someone who is the disposition or motivation of the communication (the Spirit). As the reader you are experiencing the human reflection of the diving in that these words are the communication (logos) of the author, and are given with the desire and disposition to share (spirit). This is not something I intentionally have done on my part in order to force some theological conclusion onto the experience of communication; rather, it is an observation of what is taking place. *All* human communication bears this stamp of the divine, and it gives more depth of meaning to reading, writing, listening, and speaking than we are used to thinking about. We write emails or scribble notes because we have to. Maybe some of us write stories or poetry because we feel the need to. Some of us may have a tendency to jabber aimlessly, expending words either because we want to or need to. Some people find words beautiful, but most people find words to be tools or utilities: like running water, electricity, or internet service. We know that having words makes us a little above the animals, but generally speaking the fact that we use words fills us with about as much awe as a sewage system does.

Of course, I am not saying that everyone is a potty-mouth. What I mean is that we are so used to words and communicating that it becomes as ordinary as a sink or toilet. It is so regular that we do not spend a lot of time actually thinking about it. I mean, how often have you ever used the toilet, gone away, and then a few moments later wondered if you actually flushed? If you have experienced this, then you know the terror only because using the toilet is so automatic and thoughtless. In the same way our use of words can become automatic and thoughtless. In spite of this our communication functions as a reflection of the divine. The words we produce communicate something about the communicator, whether we like it or not. This is part of the point James makes in his epistle: "Out of the same mouth proceed blessing and cursing. My brethren, these things ought not to be so."[1] Why should these things not be so? Because whether thoughtful or thoughtless, our words always communicate the soul of the communicator.

All words communicate the author or originator even as the divine Logos always communicates the Father. There is always this link between

---

1. James 3:10.

them, and this link cannot and must not be broken. No interpretation of words is valid if it does not see as the object of hearing or reading the revelation of the originator. This goes against what appears to be the popular theory of literature and communication that stipulates that the audience defines a communication's meaning. This viewpoint has become so dominant that even in a book discussing the Qur'an Jonathan A.C. Brown says, "Once you speak or write, it is the audience who decides your meaning."[2] This observation, thought truly describing man's tendency to twist ideas, is invalid when measured against the perfect Word. For when Jesus walked the earth God did not say that whatever men believed about him was a valid interpretation. No, Jesus' words were quite clear in John 8:24 when he said, ". . . if you do not believe that I am *He*, you will die in your sins." He acknowledged the fact that there were two choices available, to believe he is the I am or not to believe that, but acknowledging the choice did not validate the appropriateness of both choices. They might have called him a liar, a Samaritan, or a devil, but this did not make him any of these things. More than this, God will judge men based on whether they interpret and believe what he intended them to believe about the Logos, Jesus Christ.

Just because the audience can interpret an author's words any way does not mean it is valid to do so. We all know this intrinsically, and feel a certain level of frustration when someone (intentionally or unintentionally) does not accept or understand our words. It is frustrating because they not merely misunderstand our words, they misunderstand *us*. Whether we mean it or not we are carried by our words. Cartoonist Bill Watterson, in discussing the creation of his comic *Calvin and Hobbes* put it this way.

> Their [Calvin's and Hobbes's] words and actions are fictitious, sometimes the opposite of what I would say or do, but their emotional centers are very true to the way I think . . . Together they're pretty much a transcript of my mental diary. I didn't set out to do this, but that's what came out, and frankly it's pretty startling to read these strips and see my personality exposed so plainly right there on paper. I meant to disguise that better . . . Without exactly intending to, I learned a lot about what I love—imagination, deep friendship, animals, family, the natural world, ideas, ideals . . . and silliness . . . Giving words and form to what had previously been jumbled, half conscious thoughts, I occasionally felt like I hit some truth, and in doing so, got to know myself a little better.[3]

2. Brown, *Misquoting Muhammad*, 84.
3. Watterson. *Complete Calvin and Hobbes*, 13, 18.

Now I chose this example for a couple of important reasons. First, I chose it because *Calvin and Hobbes* is a fantastic comic, and everyone should read it. Second, because Watterson is a cartoonist and not a professional literary theorist. He is not trying to provide an explanation of why his work expressed him; he was merely observing that it had. Unintentionally, but naturally, *he* was expressed. I would dare say that the quality and popularity of the comic would have been much less had not Watterson been evident in it.

What I hope to have illustrated is that though a reader can twist and misinterpret all he wants, the word is always expressive of the author. This is because our words, however imperfectly, do what the divine Word does: expressed the one who sent him. It was bound up in who he was and is. "Lord, show us the Father," is what Philip said to Jesus. When Jesus answered it was to say, "Have I been with you so long, and yet you have not known Me, Philip? He who has seen Me has seen the Father."[4] Jesus was not just saying that he spoke what the Father wanted him to speak (though he did do this), it was that in his very person that the Father was seen and known. It would have been unthinkable for Jesus to have done anything else but communicate the Father, and what the Father intended.

Jesus, as the perfect Logos communicating the perfect being, is the archetype of imperfect human communication. The validity and quality of the imperfect is always dependant on how well it emulates the perfect. And the reality is, no matter how much we might wish it was otherwise, our words express who we are. This might not seem like an observation worthy of a chapter in a book, but a consideration of social media will illustrate the need to take seriously the nature of our words. How often are there things typed in a post, in a thread, or in a text that are something other than what we would say in person? How often do we read a post, thread, or text and marvel that it could really have been written by the person whose name is attached to it? The fingers that type can be just as awful and as untamable as the tongue. Why is this? I would suggest that when sitting behind a keyboard or a screen we feel as though our words can exist outside of ourselves as tools that are not really expressing who we are. We can be bold, defiant, rude, or deceptive without thinking anything of it, for our words are not us.

Such things happen more often than any of us would like to admit, and it happens to Christians as well. This should not be so, for to Christians all words should be seen as more than communication; they should be seen

4. John 14:8–9.

as reflections, as examples of the divine Word. When Jesus said it was not what goes into a man but what comes out that defiles him he was merely pointing out that we are as we speak, just as the Father is as the Logos presents him. Every crude word, every hateful statement, every lie tells our audience that deep down, in our most hidden heart, we are exactly those things we speak. In the same way, every time we speak the truth, every blessing we speak, every word of edification is a proclamation of who we are. This is what the Triune God teaches us as people who communicate. Our words are as God's Word: revealing the very one who speaks or writes.

This truth must also inform the recipients of communication. When we listen or read we are not simply receiving symbols; we are receiving the very person himself. When reading Bill Watterson's comic you are not just reading *Calvin and Hobbes*, you are communing with Mr. Watterson. If you enjoy the comic, you are enjoying the comic's author. If you laugh at something that Calvin or Hobbes says, you are laughing at Mr. Watterson's joke. You cannot interpret any words, whether written or spoken, outside of the author's will. I was going to say you cannot interpret any words outside of the author's *intention*, and perhaps this is the correct word, because thoughts and intentions are not always apprehended and understood completely, even by the author. By this I mean that scripture claims to be the discerner of the thoughts and intentions of the heart, indicating that one could not properly understand these things without the mirror of God's word.[5] And certainly in the heat of the moment, when a person snaps out in anger or frustration, the speaker has not put a great deal of thought into what he says. He does not reflect upon what this displays about himself, and even after he says the dreadful thing, he may not realize that it came from deep within him. One might say that his intention would normally have been otherwise, but just because a person says things in anger he would not ordinarily say in a cool moment does not negate the fact that in anger he *did* intend to say whatever came out of his mouth. So the hearer has every right to associate the angry or hurtful thing with the person. There can be no divorcing the two. There may be forgiveness, but forgiveness is not the same thing as disassociation.

The Trinitarian model of communication requires an audience to link words to the author no matter the form. Interpretation must always have, as its goal, determining what the words are communicating about the author: either what he is like or what he wants us to know. This is not an

5. Heb 4:12.

attempt to leap over the words to get into the mind of the author, but rather recognizing that the words *are* communicating the mind of the author. The beauty of fiction, history, biography, poetry, speech, joke, or song is not lost but rather enhanced when we see these things not as something existing on their own, but as an expression of his mind. Any attempt to separate the two is to diminish the word. Even when the author attempts to create something independent of himself, with no discernible intention within the content of the words, still he cannot fully escape that they communicate this about him. An author may write a poem and declare that he has no intended meaning, but even there he cannot cause the words to be something they are not, for they will still express him: incoherently to the audience perhaps, but communicated nevertheless. This is because no matter what effort is made, no matter how much sin clouds his mind, still the speaker and author bears the image of the Triune God.

There is no escaping this reality of human nature, but it can be understood, and it can only be understood properly within the Trinitarian worldview. This is how powerful the revelation of God is. This is how informative this doctrine can be. What we have been given is not only a ticket to heaven, but a way of life and a way of understanding all of life. Too often our theology stops at the doors of church buildings, in the halls of classrooms, or the pages of a theological book. But Yahweh is bigger than a building, a room, or a book. He is more alive than any study can properly understand. His fingerprints are to be found everywhere, and the key to understanding the everywhere is to understand him. He is communicated to us in written word and most importantly in the person of his Son. Jesus Christ is the King of Kings, ruling and serving as a model for all kings. He is the Lord of lords, commanding and serving as an example for all earthy lords. We have also seen that he is the perfect expression, the perfect communication of the perfect God. So in this way he is not only King of Kings and Lord of Lords, but is also the Word of words.

12

Conclusion

IT IS A PITY that the theologies of the ancient pagan gods were given by skillful poets while the theology of the living God so often comes in the dreadful prose of theologians. God would do just such a thing: choose the boring people of the world to write about the most exciting and wonderful things. But he has done this, and it is probably just as well that he did. For in this way he forces our attention away from literature to life. And the study of God must affect our lives, touching our souls in such as way that our minds are renewed and every action is influenced, no matter how great or how small.

Every generation must confront the daunting task of knowing God. It is not enough to read the accounts of men long dead, though it is important to appreciate those accounts. It is not enough to accept ancient formulations, though a long journey more often than not ends with arriving at the ancient home. The joy and power of going on such journeys is not the end, but the trip itself. Just consider Frodo and Sam at the end of the *Lord of the Rings*. There would have been nothing learned if, immediately after the Council of Elrond, the two hobbits had been lifted up by the eagles and carried to Mount Doom. There would have been no meaning in the act, no transformation of the soul that could be used for real life. Because in a sense the quest of the Ring was not real life; it was not the life that mattered dearly to the hobbits. But the truth that they realized was that this wider world was indeed the real world, and in being real it influenced how they lived in their own little Shire. This is the beauty of Tolkien's book. He used the grand to touch the small. Those last few chapters of the *Lord of the Rings* are necessary because they are the purest expression of the author's Catholic worldview. He made the little people a part, an integral part, of the grand story. He also made the grand story an integral part of the little people.

In the same way when we get a glimpse of the true nature of the grand God it touches our little lives, in our own short period of history. When we grab hold of this truth about Yahweh we enter into more than a set of beliefs and confessions. We partake of a common heritage, shared by people over thousands of years. We are a part of a people whose hope, faith, life, and perspective is shaped by identification of and with the Three-in-One. The revelation of the Trinity offers insight into the nature of redemption, creation, and man. To say that the Trinity offers us the source of our worldview is only to say that God is the source of the worldview. He is the source not only because he says to his people, "Thou shalt live this way," but because of who he is. The starting point is not to obey; it is love. The orientation of the human heart, of human thought and human society always starts with love. For this reason the first and greatest commandment is to love Yahweh. The one who is this object of love knows that to be ignorant of the beloved is to be limited in love. So he has revealed himself in all of his mystery and strangeness.

The highest and most intimate revelation God has made of himself is the Trinity. Since God is holy, since he is other, and since he is not a man this particular revelation is so very strange to us, so controversial, and so scandalous. The controversy does not lie in the evidence. As has been shown, the evidence is clear and abundant. Rather, the controversy lies in its importance. It is a scandal to the ecumenical mind that such a doctrine should become so central a confession. It is a scandal to the ecclesiastical mind that the nature of God should become largely irrelevant to the life of the church—irrelevant to life itself!

Those who love local churches may be tempted to justify downplaying the Trinity for the sake of unity, for the sake of interacting with other people groups, or for the sake of talking about aspects of Christianity that actually seem to address how we live and why we live. This temptation must be overcome, because while it may originate in a heart of good intentions, it is the kind of thing that leads one away from God. Why? Because what results is a disregard for what God has told us about himself. It is to abandon the only unifying principle in all of redemption and all of history. To treat the doctrine of the Trinity as merely a piece of historical confession, a relic of Christian ancestors, is to miss the beauty not only of the church, but of God.

I know that I have done a poor job in communicating the wonder, the beauty, and the power of God's nature. It is too high, too lofty for me. The potency of its truth is too much for me grasp! It is like the sun that I see in the sky, that I feel, that I love and fear. I understand the sun and the basics of its workings, and I know that if harnessed there is such great power to be had. Alas, I can only offer faint descriptions of how it might be used. Yet this I know, the God whom I contemplate in my weak way is a blaze of holiness, whose rays have touched my upturned face and driven back the darkness of my heart. I cannot wait until that day when the Spirit swells within me, and my Savior leads me on with countless others, and presents us to the Father of lights. Then I know, with all that is within me, I shall join the thunderous chorus of men and angels, seraphim and cherubim, of stars and planets, of winds and rains, of rocks and trees and countless other things in that song that is forever wondrous and forever true: Holy, holy, holy, Lord God Almighty, merciful and mighty, God in three persons, blessed Trinity!

Bibliography

Assmann, Jan. *Akhenaten to Moses: Ancient Egypt and Religious Change*. Cairo: American University in Cairo Press, 2014.

—. *Of God and Gods: Egypt, Israel, and the Rise of Monotheism*. Madison: University of Wisconsin Press, 2008.

"Athenasian Creed." In *The Creeds of Christendom with A Historical and Critical Notes Volume II*, edited by Philip Schaff, 66-71. New York: Harper and Brothers, 1919.

Augustine. *On the Trinity*. Translated by Rev. Arthur West Haddan. Coppel, TX: Veritatis Splendor, 2012.

Bavink, Herman. *Reformed Dogmatics: Abridged in One Volume*. Edited by John Bolt. Grand Rapids: Baker Academic, 2008.

Beecher, Willis J. *The Prophets and the Promise*. New York: Thomas Y. Crowell, 1905. Digitized by Ted Hildebrandt at Gordon College, 2005. http://faculty.gordon.edu/hu/bi/ted_hildebrandt/otesources/23a-prophets/beecher-prophets-promise/beecher-prophetspromise.htm.

Boot, Joseph. *The Mission of God: A Manifesto of Hope for Society*. London: Wilberforce, 2016.

Borwning, Elizabeth Barrett. "The Dead Pan." *Elizabeth Barrett Browning Archive*. ebbarchive.org.

Brown, Jonathan A. C. *Misquoting Muhammad: The Challenge and Choices of Interpreting the Prophet's Legacy*. London: One World, 2014.

Chesterton, G. K. *Heretics*. In *The Collected Works of G.K. Chesterton: Volume I*, edited by David Dolley, 5–71. San Francisco: Ignatius, 1986.

—. *Orthodoxy*. In *The Collected Works Volume I*, edited by David Dolley, 76–136. San Francisco: Ignatius, 1986.

—. *The Napoleon of Notting Hill*. In *The Collected Works Volume VI*, edited by Denis J. Conlin. San Francisco: Ignatius, 1991.

Crichton, Michael. *Sphere*. New York: Alfred A. Knopf, 1987.

Dise, Robert L. *Empires Before Alexander: Course Guidebook*. Chantilly: The Great Courses, 2009.

Dixon, Larry. "The Other Comforter: The Place of the Holy Spirit in the Trinity." *The Emmaus Journal* 13 (2004) 73–119.

Edwards, Jonathan. "Discourse on the Trinity." In *The Trinitarian Theology of Jonathan Edwards*, edited by Steven M. Studebaker and Robert W. Caldwell, 23–41. London: Taylor and Francis, 2012.

Bibliography

———. "Of God the Father." *Sermons and Discourses, 1743–1758. WJE Online Volume 25* edited by Wilson H. Kimnach, 145–51.

———. "Sinners in the Hands of an Angry God: A Sermon Preached at Enfield, July 8th, 1741." *Electronic Texts in American Studies.* Edited by Reiner Smolinski. https:// digitalcommons.unl.edu/etas.

Feinberg, John S. *No One Like Him: The Doctrine of God.* Wheaton, IL: Crossway, 2001.

Ferguson, Everett. *Church History, Volume I: From Christ to the Pre-Reformation.* Grand Rapids: Zondervan, 2013.

Frankfort, Henri. *Ancient Egyptian Religion: An Interpretation.* New York: Dover, 2000.

Glover, Linda K. et al. *National Geographic Encyclopedia of Space.* Washington, DC: National Geographic, 2005.

Gonzalez, Justo L. *A History of Christian Thought: Volume I.* Nashville: Abingdon, 1987.

Grudem, Wayne. *Systematic Theology: An Introduction to Biblical Doctrine.* Grand Rapids: Zondervan, 2000.

Harris, Sam. *The Moral Landscape: How Science Can Determine Human Values.* New York: Free, 2010.

Henny, Ally. "Have You Left Yet?" *The Witness.* https://thewitnessbcc.com/why-havent-you-left-yet/.

Herodotus. *Histories.* In *The Greek Historians: Volume 1,* edited by Francis R. B. Goldolphin. New York: Random House,1942.

Hiebert, Paul G. *Transforming Worldviews: An Anthropological Understanding of How People Change.* Grand Rapids: Baker Academic, 2008.

Hill, Andrew, and John Walton. *A Survey of the Old Testament.* Grand Rapids: Zondervan, 2009.

Hodge, A.A. *Outlines of Theology.* New York: Robert Carter and Brothers, 1866.

Kaiser, Walter C., Jr. *The Promise-Plan of God: A Biblical Theology of the Old and New Testaments.* Grand Rapids: Zondervan, 2008.

Lactantius. "The Wrath of God." In *The Minor Works: The Fathers of the Church, Volume 54,* translated by Sister Mary Francis McDonald. Washington, DC: Catholic University of America Press, 1965.

Lewis, C.S. *The Lion, the Witch, and the Wardrobe.* London: Diamond, 1998.

———. *Miracles.* In *The Complete C.S. Lewis Signatures Classics.* New York: HarperOne, 2007.

———. *Mere Christianity.* In *The Complete C.S. Lewis Signature Classics.* New York: HarperOne, 2007.

Magnetti, Donald L. "The Function of the Oath in the Ancient Near Eastern International Treaty." *The American Journal of International Law* 72 (1978) 815–29.

Maharaj, Rabi R. *Death of a Guru.* Eugene, OR: Harvest House, 1984.

Melito of Sardis. "A Homily on Passover." In *The Christological Controversy,* edited by Richard A. Norris, 33–47. Philadelphia: Fortress, 1980.

Naugle, David K. *Worldview: The History of a Concept.* Grand Rapids: Eerdmans, 2002.

Noll, Mark A. *The Scandal of the Evangelical Mind.* Grand Rapids: Eerdmans, 1994.

Owen, John. *Of the Mortification of Sin in Believers.* In *Overcoming Sin and Temptation,* edited by Kelly M. Kapic and Justin Taylor. Wheaton: Crossway, 2006.

Plutarch. *Isis and Osiris.* https://penelope.uchicago.edu/Thayer/e/roman/texts/plutarch/moralia/isis_and_osiris*/a.html.

Reed, Jeff. *The Paradigm Papers.* Ames, IA: BILD International, 2017.

Rogusa, Daniel. "The Trinity at the Center of Thought and Life: Herman Bavinck's Organic Apologetic." *Mid-American Journal of Theology* 28 (2017) 149–75.

Ryrie, Charles C. *The Holy Spirit*. Chicago: Moody, 1997.

Sahih Bukhari. "Merits of Sunnah." https://www.sahih-bukhari.com/Pages/Bukhari_4_56.php.

Schwemer, Daniel "The Storm-Gods of the Ancient Near East: Summary, Synthesis, Recent Studies." *Journal of Ancient Near Eastern Religions* 7 (2007) 121–68.

Sire, James. *The Universe Next Door*. Downers Grove: IVP Academic, 2009.

Sire, James. *Naming the Elephant*. Downers Grove: IVP Academic, 2015.

Sproul, R.C. *The Holiness of God*. Carol Stream, IL: Tyndale House, 1998.

Tennent, Timothy C. "The Bible and Islam." *Crossway Articles*. https://www.crossway.org/articles/the-bible-and-islam/.

Tolkien, J.R.R. *The Lord of the Rings*. Boston: Houghton Mifflin, 1987.

Walton, John. *Ancient Near Eastern Thought and the Old Testament: Introducing the Conceptual World of the Hebrew Bible*. Grand Rapids: Baker Academic, 2006.

Ware, Bruce A. *Father, Son, and Holy Spirit: Relationships, Roles, and Relevance*. Wheaton: Crossway, 2005.

Warfield, B.B. "The Person of Christ." *The Life, Thought, and Works of Benjamin Breckinridge Warfield (1851–1921)*. http://bbwarfield.com/works/person-of-christ/.

———. "Trinity." *The Life, Thought, and Works of Benjamin Breckinridge Warfield (1851–1921)*. bbwarfield.com/works/trinity.

Watson, Thomas. *Body of Divinity*. In *The Select Works of the Reverend Thomas Watson Comprising His Celebrated Body of Divinity in a Series of Lectures on the Shorter Catechism, and Various Sermons and Treaties*. New York: Robert Carter and Brothers, 1855.

Watterson, Bill. *The Complete Calvin and Hobbes: Book One*. Kansas City: Andrews McMeel, 2017.

White, James R. *The Forgotten Trinity*. Minneapolis: Bethany House, 1998.

Wilkinson, Richard H. *The Complete Gods and Goddesses of Ancient Egypt*. London: Thames and Hudson, 2003.

Wilson, Douglas and James White. "The Trinity and Patriarchy." *Sweater Vest Dialogues*. https://www.youtube.com/watch?v=bdANHJFRJuM.